CHILD LABOUR

This book is for Anna-Maria
in the confident expectation that
she will never have to labour at
the expense of her development

CHILD LABOUR

Alec Fyfe

Polity Press

Copyright © Alec Fyfe 1989

First published 1989 by Polity Press
in association with Basil Blackwell

Editorial office:
Polity Press, 65 Bridge Street,
Cambridge CB2 1UR, UK

Marketing and production:
Basil Blackwell Ltd
108 Cowley Road, Oxford, OX4 1JF, UK

Basil Blackwell Inc.
3 Cambridge Center
Cambridge, MA 02142, USA

ISBN 0 7456 03998
ISBN 0 7456 04005 (pbk)

British Library Cataloguing in Publication Data
A CIP catalogue record for this book is available from the British
Library

Typeset in 11 on 13 pt Baskerville
by Joshua Associates Ltd, Oxford
Printed in Great Britain by
T.J. Press, Padstow

Contents

Acknowledgements

My interest in child labour began in 1983 when I helped initiate a project between UNICEF(UK), for whom I worked as their Education Officer, and the TUC. Out of this joint venture emerged in 1985 the educational publication *All Work and No Play: Child Labour Today*. That most satisfying experience would not have been possible but for the support of John Greystone and Pauline Ortiz, then members of the TUC's Education and International Departments respectively. At the end of 1985 I was commissioned by the International Labour Organization (ILO) to produce a paper on campaigning strategies which forms the basis of chapter 6 of this book. Here I am indebted to Assefa Bequele of the ILO and in particular to Richard Tames of the School of Oriental and African Studies (SOAS) who suggested the outline of the Child Labour Campaign Model. My major professional debt in this field continues to be owed to Judith Ennew. I have drawn extensively upon Judith's work on child labour, street children and child prostitution that she undertook during her association with the Anti-Slavery Society. My thanks to UNICEF(UK) who supported my original work with the TUC and for access to documents and photographs. Finally, as always, a special thanks to Esther Valdivia who produced the numerous drafts and the final typescript. All this was done under the most difficult of circumstances when she was labouring in the production and then care of our daughter, to whom this book is dedicated.

Alec Fyfe
Winchester
25 November, 1988

Introduction

In recent years there has been a growing interest in child labour among academics, professionals and the media. This book attempts to bring the whole field up to date and to provide a comprehensive introduction for the specialist and general reader. In pursuing this aim I try to move beyond a narrative account and to offer an analysis of the underlying causes of child labour world-wide and its consequences for children and society at large. Throughout there is a focus on policy matters, and on what can be accomplished at national and international levels to confront this most neglected of public policy issues.

Child labour is prohibited in virtually all countries, and yet it continues to flourish, and indeed may be a growing phenomenon with economic recession in industrialized countries and persistent poverty in developing countries. And though it is through work that most children are exploited world-wide, nowhere does child labour feature high on the priority list of governmental and inter-governmental agencies. It was only during the International Year of the Child (IYC, 1979) that international attention became fully focused on the problem of child labour. Prior to IYC child labour had been the subject of national action and, through the International Labour Organization (ILO), of a growing attempt at international standard setting.

Awareness of the harmful effects of child labour first occurred in industrialized countries during the last century. Child labour was reduced and then virtually eliminated by the early part of this century through a combination of economic changes, which decreased the demand for child workers, and the introduction of universal schooling, which absorbed the supply of children for work. Where children continue to work in advanced industrialized countries it is usually in a part-time capacity. Few, if any, children in Europe and North America work out of absolute economic necessity. Despite official disinterest in the subject, children, particularly of ethnic minority groups, like gypsies, do engage in illegal work and are exposed to unhealthy and unsafe working conditions. When it comes to child prostitution and pornography some industrial countries are world leaders. The fact that millions of children work, most of them illegally and some of them to the detriment of their health and development, contradicts the popular mythology that child labour is a thing of the past. This myth has been sustained in Britain through the continuous retelling of the romantic story of the freeing of 'child slaves' by Lord Shaftesbury in Victorian England. Indeed, the first campaigns against child labour did take place in England in the 1830s and 1840s and they mark a historic shift in thinking about the proper role of children and childhood itself. Out of the moral crisis presented by child labour emerged the view of the 'innocent child' (but also of the savage child) whose rightful place was in the school room. The perpetuation of this myth by the rescuing agency itself reveals the extent to which the medium has become the message. This Western notion of childhood has now become a pervasive one through cultural transfer to the developing world.

In developing countries the vast majority of children continue to contribute to the family economy, as was the case in all societies prior to the last century. According to Professor Boudhiba, who was asked to produce the first report on child labour for the United Nations, nearly 98 per cent of working children are found in the developing world (Boudhiba, 1982). Here child labour not only remains economically important, but it is on the whole as morally unquestioned as was the case in Britain before the end of the eighteenth century. Child work is often regarded as natural and is therefore accorded a low priority within government agencies, workers' and employers' associations. As child labour is often illegal there is also a widespread attempt, by parents, employers and the children themselves, to conceal it. The worst abuses easily go undetected and there is a surprisingly high degree of ignorance

about the consequences of child labour for children, the economy
and society at large. The facts about child labour, particularly the
extent of the problem, are difficult to establish. Boudhiba thought
145 million children worked world-wide but this is really a
guesstimate.

There is little room for complacency in believing that the problem
of child labour is being significantly reduced. For example, in Nepal,
there has been a steady rise over the last 30 years in the proportion of
children aged between 10 and 14 years engaged in work: from 28 per
cent in 1952–4 to 50 per cent in 1971, and to 58 per cent in 1981
(Ideas Forum, 1985). Asia has the largest number of child workers in
the world. In India alone, there are an estimated 17.36 million child
workers, comprising 5.9 per cent of the labour force. Nevertheless,
the highest proportion of child workers in relation to the total child
population is to be found in Africa. As many as 20 per cent of
children may be working, with child workers constituting as much
as 17 per cent of the work-force in some African countries. In Latin
America the problem is on a smaller scale with perhaps 2 to 5 per
cent as the official range, although other estimates suggest a higher
figure of 12–26 per cent (ILO, 1985). Latin America also has the
highest incidence of children working in the urban informal sector.
These 'street children' are some of the worst abused and exploited
children in the world today. Though most working children are still
found in the rural areas, it is rapid urbanization that gives rise to
growing international concern because of its association with work
outside of the family context. However, as I show in the book, one
should not be blind to the fact that parents can and do exploit their
own children.

In going beyond the measurement of child work to an analysis of
causes and consequences it is customary to begin with those
definitional conundrums: *what is a child? what is work? what is
exploitation?* It is these fundamental imprecisions that are often
thought to deflect attention from what is objectively a serious and a
growing problem. In jumping through these traditional hoops I take
the view in the book that we need to make a basic distinction
between 'child work' and 'child labour'. These concepts are usually
used interchangeably in the literature. This has led to much
confusion and a failure to focus and mobilize significant attention on
the real priorities within the field. Clearly, not all work is bad for
children. This view commands almost universal agreement. There is

little doubt that many children welcome the opportunity to work, seeing in it the rite of passage to adulthood. Work can be a gradual intiation into adulthood and a positive element in the child's development. Light work, properly structured and phased, is not child labour. Work which does not detract from the other essential activities for children, namely leisure, play and education, is not child labour. Child labour is work which impairs the health and development of children. There should be little argument about what constitutes the super-exploitation of children through work. Priority ought to go to the targeting and rooting out of child prostitution, child pornography, bonded and tied labour, and work in hazardous occupations, including military service. But exploitation is not a concept that can be given a precise objective meaning. We can identify the extremes – children working in slave-like conditions in factories and mines, using dangerous chemicals in pesticide-soaked fields, imprisoned in homes as domestic servants, working as prostitutes, or in guerilla armies. At the margins, though, there will always be a subjective facet; exploitation will lie in the eye of the beholder.

Children work because their work has important social and economic functions. Both factors are interrelated in the causal chain which determines the level of demand for children's work, its supply, and the form that work takes. In terms of economic factors, two determinants can be identified: first, the nature of the production process, and second, the structure of the labour market (Rodgers and Standing, 1981, p. 13). In pre-capitalist simple societies exploitative relationships can be identified both within the independent peasant family system, and in lineage modes of production where groups receive surplus production out of social obligation. Forms of debt bondage, fostering and adoption may all reflect 'feudal' relationships in which children are viewed as producers. Within this sytem of work sharing and steady integration into adult tasks and obligations, schooling has little value.

The transition to industrial capitalism has been associated in the industrialized countries with a long-term decline in child employment. Nevertheless, during the early part of the industrial revolution in Britain children were used more intensively. Whole families were hired for a 'family wage' based upon the calculation of output from all its members. In most developing countries today children are not found in large firms, but work in small manufacturing enterprises as cheap 'sweated' labour, often not for a direct wage but for a 'supplementary wage' which goes to the parent worker. Technical innovation in the urban sector, which has no place for children, often forces children into street trades turning child labour into casual labour. Rural to urban migration, itself a common feature of the transition to capitalism, means in some cases that it is the women and children who are left to perform more intensively the domestic and income earning agricultural work. The move to a capitalist mode of production also radically changes the labour market, typically in the direction of greater fragmentation. The use of child workers fits well into such a system. Unorganized, with few dependents, no rights, a need for income, and vulnerable by their very nature, children are the most readily exploited of all labour groups. Their low cost gives to the employer a potential competitive advantage, both in the domestic and export market. The growth of the wage labour market greatly increases the significance of schooling. But the access to schooling is itself differentiated, with poor families constrained by the direct and indirect costs of education. Poor children face a permanent disadvantage in the labour market. The drift to urban areas in the early stages of industrialization is usually associated with high unemployment which forces many families and their children to eke out a living in marginal, casual forms of employment.

Child work not only responds to economic forces; it reflects social and cultural patterns, including power relationships between adults and children. The roles of children are associated with the values attached to children, while 'childhood' is itself a social construct. Gender roles in childhood help prepare for an adult sexual division of labour in which females are more intensively involved in domestic activities. Domestic organization and the type of family system have their related sets of rights and obligations. These are adult rights over children and reflect the social construction of an age hierarchy (Elson, 1982, p. 491). The subordinate status of children is universal, whether it be as producers in developing societies or as economic dependents in industrialized societies. The implications of this analysis is to move the focus of policy discussion away from an exclusive preoccupation with protection towards a greater consideration of enhancing children's rights and the development of their capacities for self-determination (Elson, 1982, p. 494).

We should be conscious of the dangers of imposing our Western values on other societies, in particular our notions of 'normal' childhood and child development. This often leads outsiders into 'shock-horror' reactions to child work in developing countries and resultant over-idealistic and impractical recommendations for action. The predictable response from most governments has been to ignore such hectoring. Not surprisingly then, the most comprehensive international child labour standard, the ILO Convention 138 (1973), has had a poor take-up. There has also been relatively little interest shown by developing countries in the drafting of the UN Convention on the Rights of the Child.

In response to this current policy and programme impasse I shall be suggesting that there is a need for a more pragmatic and focused approach to the setting of priorities. The first priority ought to be the elimination of the super-exploitation of children through work. These forms are easy to identify, are relatively less well defended by entrenched interest, and are more likely to carry the potential for popular mobilization in opposition to them. In practice, this will mean in the short term concentrating largely on the urban sector. This does not imply ignoring the rural areas, but pragmatically they are a second order priority. It also means finding ways of creatively combining work and welfare services, including education. Attempts at abolishing child work at a stroke without compensatory improvements in income and welfare provision would only leave poor families worse off.

Another practical reason for concentrating on the urban areas is that they are more likely to contain organized labour. An important emphasis in this book is the potential role trade unions can play in the campaign against child labour. Boudhiba suggested this in his report but unfortunately the challenge has not been taken up in any significant way. Trade unions do have the potential to cut through the current Gordian knot of inertia which binds the issue. They can detect abuses, lobby governments to adopt and then to adhere to international labour standards, and can organize those marginal groups who are more dependent upon child labour. But it is their capacity for campaigning that is most crucial. Public education is universally agreed to be the first significant step along the road to the eradication of child labour. This book presents for the first time a model of how such public awareness campaigns could be constructed. Though I see trade unions at the centre of such campaigns it has to be acknowledged that historically trade unions have not taken a great deal of interest in the issue. Trade unions tend to face the same dilemmas as governments, in that they respond to what is still seen as an economic necessity for poor families. Of course, the real underlying cause of child labour is the widespread poverty found in developing countries and within regions in industrialized countries.

Drawing attention to the underlying factors of poverty and inequality ought to be central to child labour campaigning. In this book I contend that the UN system has a crucial responsibility for co-operating with the non-governmental community, and with government agencies, to utilize the considerable potential which exists for public education campaigns. This could begin with pilot projects in the use of trade union education programmes and the mass media. The ILO as the lead agency in the labour field, and the United Nations Children's Fund (UNICEF), as the predominant agency for child welfare, are best placed to sponsor such experimentation, but other UN agencies also have a role to play, especially the United Nations Educational Scientific and Cultural Organization (UNESCO), the World Health Organization (WHO), the United Nations Development Programme (UNDP), and the Food and Agricultural Organization (FAO). Unfortunately, this kind of agency co-operation, though often recommended, is difficult to achieve. The problem of child labour demands a more integrated approach, as do other development issues. Children cannot be neatly parcelled up between a variety of separate agencies.

The whole UN system has, in recent years, been facing the worst crisis since its inception, and often gives the impression of being the greatest black hole in the universe – so many good intentions and resources poured in to little effect! However, it ought to be pointed out to its critics that, in the words of Dag Hammarskjöld, the UN is there not to bring mankind to heaven but to save it from hell and, like the cleric during the French Revolution, its greatest achievement may well be to have survived and to go on surviving. It must be remembered, too, that we get the international system we deserve. If child labour is not a high priority for the ILO and UNICEF it is largely because member states wish it to be so. Child labour is an issue which quickly gets to the heart of the development problem of poverty and inequality.

In 1985 I had a unique opportunity to witness how the UN system responds to child labour. The first ever UN Seminar on Child

Labour was held in Geneva between 28 October and 8 November 1985, and I had the privilege of presenting UNICEF's paper. The Seminar was one of the recommendations of the Bouhdiba report and it attracted 24 government representatives, with additional participation from UN and non-governmental agencies. The absences on the UN side were glaring. Despite the fact that most child work takes place in agriculture, the FAO failed to attend; and despite the fact that schooling is universally viewed as the antidote to work, UNESCO failed to send a representative. So much for global solidarity with children, which was the plea from the ILO at the opening of the Seminar.

It must be said that the two weeks which followed were not the most edifying, but were instructive in the ways of the UN. Of course, Geneva itself is bound to lend any such proceedings a sense of unreality. It is difficult to focus on poverty in the richest country in Europe which is itself staunchly independent of the UN. In no real sense was the occasion a seminar: government representatives came to present set positions which made for a sterile ritual. No session ever started on time and the whole proceedings could have been half the length. The sub-texts of such events are usually more significant and entertaining. Predictably the socialist states had already consigned the problem of child labour in their own countries to the scrap heap of history. In a kind of socialist genesis the USSR asserted that on 'the fifth day after the October Revolution' they passed a law abolishing child labour. Children who now appear in Soviet factories are there as guests. Nevertheless the time-honoured practice of using schoolchildren to help bring in the harvest seems to persist. A Reuter report of 1987 mentioned thousands of children in the Soviet Central Asian Republic of Turkmenia being taken from their classes to help with the cotton harvest in open defiance of a Party ruling (*Independent*, 31 October 1987). In similar vein the People's Republic of China referred to child labour as having 'become history' in their country. But nearly three years later the *People's Daily* was claiming that children as young as ten represented up to 20 per cent of the work-force in certain rural industries and the labour minister was launching a child labour campaign (AFP, 26 May 1988). *Glasnost* was still in the future and such ideological 'at-a-stroke' positions allowed the socialist states to put themselves conveniently, in the words of the German Democratic Republic, in the van of the 'progressive forces fighting child labour'.

It is almost too prosaic to state that child labour is not going to be abolished by seminars, campaigns or projects, but only through a concerted attack on poverty – the absolute poverty where work is necessary for survival, and the relative poverty of the need to work in order to participate fully in the normal life of the community. Child labour is one index of the extent of poverty and inequality in all societies. In most societies, most children do not have the choice about whether they work or not, or under what conditions that work takes place. In advanced industrialized countries there are those within the counter culture who claim that children are denied the right to work. This is the final twist in the tail of this most complex issue. Child labour has in recent years become part of the human rights domain.

The context of the Boudhiba report was the Commission on Human Rights, as was the UN Seminar. The Draft of the UN Convention on the Rights of the Child itself has a clause on child labour. Child liberationists see many dangers in an over-protective approach to children and would have them exercising the same rights as adults, including that of being able to join trade unions. There has been talk too of child workers exercising self-organization to promote their concerns, as has occurred to a limited extent in Brazil and Peru. Though there are difficulties with an overly paternalistic approach, children are a special category, and there will, and must be, a strong protective aspect to the relationship between children and adults. Nevertheless, this protection should be exercised in such a way that it facilitates the growing autonomy and development of children. I do not think this is a contradiction. Debates about children's rights must seem frivolous and an indulgence to the millions of labouring children in the developing world. Too much energy and time should not be fruitlessly spent on trying to determine how many 'autonomous' and 'self-organizing' children can dance on the point of a needle! Rather there is a need to strike a balance between the protection of children and the participation of children in change.

The real need is to devise strategies which recognize the reality that in the forseeable future most children, in most societies, will still need to work to support themselves and their families. The international community must go beyond the hand-wringing response of moral outrage to a calm and objective assessment of practical and realizable objectives. This means devising ways of humanizing the work of children by combining it creatively with education, health and welfare services. Children as workers ought to be covered by the same regulations concerning health, safety and wages as those which apply to adult workers, including the right to belong to free trade unions. Ultimately, children should have the right to the choice of whether they work or not. This book is a modest contribution to greater international understanding of this highly complex and much neglected humanitarian issue. If the persistence of child labour is an affront to the world community (Blanchard, 1983) then the mobilization of a global campaign is now long overdue.

To this end I begin the book by exploring the concepts raised by the issue, particularly the central distinction between child work and child labour, before examining the effects of exploitative work on children and society. This context-setting chapter is followed by two chapters on Europe and the USA which aim to dispel the myth that child labour is a thing of the past in industrialized societies. For analytic purposes the two following chapters on the developing world are divided firstly into examining child labour in terms of causes and patterns in the rural context and then in the urban setting. Chapter 6 deals in greater depth with policy issues and in particular with the potential for constructing campaigns against child labour. The final chapter reviews public policy issues before exploring child labour in a human rights context and the ethical dilemmas it raises.

1

The Meaning and Consequences of Child Labour

'What I want is FACTS . . . Facts alone are wanted in life.'
Charles Dickens, *Hard Times*

How many children work in the world today? Establishing this simple fact and much else about the meaning and consequences of child work is not as easy as it might appear. Dickens's Mr Gradgrind would be driven to apoplexy by the plethora of estimates or guesstimates in the field. Recent commentators start with the 1979 ILO figure of 52 million. However, in 1983 ILO called this a conservative estimate. For one thing it only included full-time workers. The Anti-Slavery Society estimates that the figure is more like 100 million (1985, p. 7). Professor Boudhiba suggested in his report to the UN that 145 million working children between the age of 10 and 14 was more realistic.

The regional picture is not much clearer. Asia is thought to have the largest child worker population. India alone is officially said to have 17.36 million child workers, more than anywhere else, comprising 5.9 per cent of the total labour force – some 93 per cent of these child workers are in the rural areas (UN Seminar, 1985); and yet, other estimates for India talk of 54 million and 100 million. In Africa, 20 per cent of children under 15 are said to be working, and in some African cities, children constitute 17 per cent of the total work-force. In Latin America, estimates between 12 and 26 per cent have been put forward for some countries (ILO paper, UN Seminar, 1985).

Clearly much more rigorous work needs to be done in this area, but it is in no state's interest to have an accurate picture of the extent of child work, and only recently has the subject attracted social scientists. If we are to attain a better understanding of child work then we shall need to place it within the broader framework of the institution of childhood which has attracted the attention of historians, sociologists and anthropologists. Here one is reminded of Anna Freud's depiction of childhood as a phenomenon which taxed or defied our understanding. Nevertheless, it would be useful to explore childhood in an historical context, at least to begin with, in order to obtain a view on how we have arrived at the various perceptions of what is desirable or undesirable for children.

It was Philippe Ariès in his classic *Centuries of Childhood*, who first put forward the thesis that childhood is a modern Western invention. According to Ariès, 'there was no place for childhood in the medieval world' (Jenks, 1982, p. 31). The infant who could not participate in the adult world simply did not count. Only gradually in the sixteenth and seventeenth centuries do we witness, in the art of the times, the child or infant of the upper strata depicted in special dress and thereby distinguished from adults. By the eighteenth century everything to do with children's health and education had become established as a concern worthy of serious attention. By the end of that century childhood had been established by Blake and Wordsworth as a major literary theme, something which was to continue well into the nineteenth century with Dickens, Mark Twain and Tolstoy.

The seventeenth century appears then as a watershed in the evolution of the modern institution of childhood. 'Baby', 'child' and 'youth' were interchangeable terms prior to the modern age. The child in medieval society was fully integrated from the earliest age into all aspects of daily life including education, work and play. Children were treated as if they were expendable, as indeed they were. Even in the early nineteenth century the English essayist Charles Lamb could remark in a letter to a friend '. . . we have had a sick child, who, sleeping or not sleeping, next to me, with a pasteboard partition between, killed my sleep. The little bastard is gone' (Schorsch, 1979, p. 11). At the end of the fifteenth century the numbers seven and fourteen were already associated with child-hood. Seven was the beginning of the rite of passage for boys, when apprenticeship contracts were drawn up, and by 14 schooling in reading, writing and religion was over, as was apprenticeship. Girls were even less likely to survive infancy and were regarded as a liability by medieval parents until married off as early as 12 (if a sufficently attractive dowry could be provided). Girls were less likely to have been schooled and would remain subordinated to men throughout life. The Reformation, with its encouragement of individualism, also helped to establish the individuality of the child. By the end of the seventeenth century each child was regarded as having a soul of its own and was given its own name. This separation had its price in the growing institutional constraints on the child's freedom. Parents, the Church, moralists, and educators all came to circumscribe the world of the child, who was deemed to need both protection and a prolonged period of training.

Today we have come a long way from the romantic view of innocent childhood in which children were depicted as 'little angels' who are 'closer to God'. Today childhood in industrialized countries is problematic, protracted, ill-defined, and the centre of vehement claims and counter-claims concerning 'what is best for the child.' Childhood has spawned an army of child-care professional experts in the new sciences of pedagogy, paediatrics, psychology and psychoanalysis (Ennew, 1986a). The modern conception of childhood, invented and sustained by adults, has two key features. Firstly, a rigid age hierarchy which separates children from adults. This institutionalization of childhood is marked by special dress, games, language and literature. Secondly, the myth of childhood innocence where the child must be both happy and separated from the corrupt adult world. This becomes expressed in the child-centred family which is determined materially, if in no other way, to make these the best years of life.

These adult modes and prescriptions have been codified into international standards expressed in Declarations, Covenants and Charters. These date back to the early part of this century and express a protective view of childhood. In such instruments the child cannot by definition be a worker in the formal economy, but requires a protracted period of socialization in which schooling becomes the acceptable form of 'work' for the child. Children have become in these circumstances economic dependants and liabilities. And school-days are seen as a golden age.

Nevertheless, there are physiological criteria which provide clear broad stages in childhood and its separation from adulthood. These are: infancy (0–5), pre-pubertal childhood (6–12), and post-pubertal childhood (12 to adulthood or majority). The age of adulthood is now expressed by the Draft UN Convention on the Rights of the Child as 'being eighteen unless, under the law of his/her state he/she has reached his/her age of majority earlier.' In the end one returns to the simplest of all definitions of a child by chronological age which itself differs from state to state.

Children have always worked and today where families need help, in developed and developing countries, children will and do continue to work. Work has always been part of a wider set of childhood activities which is the starting point for any classificiation and analysis of children's economic role. Here the most comprehensive conceptual framework to date is that of Rodgers and Standing. The authors distinguish ten childhood activities: domestic work; non-domestic work; non-monetary work; tied or bonded labour; wage labour; marginal economic activities; schooling; idleness and unemployment; recreation and leisure; and reproductive activities (Rodgers and Standing, 1981, pp. 2–11).

Typically, cooking, cleaning, child care and other domestic duties are under taken to some extent by children in all societies. Such duties form part of the socialization process and cannot, according to the International Labour Organization, be termed child labour (Blanchard, 1983, p. 18). But domestic work, as it has been defined, becomes 'social exploitation' if it denies children their right to play, to learn and to enjoy a normal childhood. Many children, especially girls, do miss educational and recreational opportunities because of a heavy domestic work burden. Though domestic work does not of itself produce an income it is economically important because it facilitates adult work, freeing parents to go out to earn money. Such domestic work can begin very early, especially in developing countries, where the starting age can be as low as five or less. Though girls often carry the heaviest burden of preparing food, cleaning the house, washing the clothes and looking after younger brothers and sisters, boys too, in countries as diverse as Peru, Jamaica and India, play their part (see figure 1.1).

Nevertheless, boys tend to do less, particularly in the case of child care, though there are examples where pre-pubertal boys share domestic duties with girls. But not all domestic work takes place within the child's own family. There are the 'maids-of-all-work' in developing countries, whom Professor Boudhiba described as

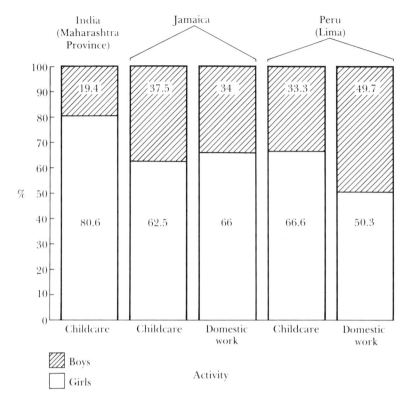

Figure 1.1   Childcare and domestic work performed by minors,
related to sex of worker in three countries
Sources: Ennew and Young, 1981; Ennew, 1985; Shah et al.,
ASS, 1984, p. 146

virtual slaves (Boudhiba, 1982, p. 46). These girls tend to come from
rural areas to the home of an urban 'relative' who undertakes to look
after them and provide them with an education. But they are usually
being farmed out to distant, if not fictional, relatives where they need
not be paid for being on call virtually 24 hours a day. Being strangers
to the city and isolated from their parents, they are powerless to
change their position. Domestic work is not only an unrecognized
form of economic contribution, it remains unappreciated as a form
of child labour.

   Non-domestic, non-monetary work forms a continuum with
domestic work, especially in subsistence economies. It encompasses
such time-consuming activities as looking after animals, protecting

fields from pests, weeding, etc. Analytically, this category can be broken down depending on whether the production is for the family's consumption or for the market, and whether the child is working for its own benefit, or for parents, for relatives, or for strangers. This form of child work for no pay is widely viewed as the largest sector of child work in the world. At the first UN Seminar on Child Labour, delegates from developing countries stressed that this type of work expressed family solidarity and therefore was not subject to exploitative relationships. Exploitation occurs, they contended, when third parties are involved, usually in an urban context. Thus, logically, child labour cannot be a major problem. The anthropological evidence, though non-quantitative, tends to undermine this blithe assumption. The idea that rural children learn as they work and are, therefore, experiencing a traditional form of socialization rather than exploitation, ignores the extent to which even simple societies are now integrated into cash economies and are subject to agricultural capitalism. In reality, children are involved from the age of five or six in hard labour in agrarian communities. One study of family labour among pastoralists in the Sahel has shown that children often perform much harder work than adults and such work often expresses a sexual division of labour: 'The boys look after the sheep, gather wood, collect fodder, draw water, sow and reap. The girls milk, cook, spin, look after the younger children. The country child is invariably a working child and work is a fundamental part of his/her existence' (Mendelievich, 1979, p. 128).

Such work demands often prelcude school attendance; besides, much of the curricula is urban biased and Western orientated, which often acts as a further inducement for parents to see their children working rather than wasting their time in irrelevant study. This social exploitation results in a lifetime disadvantage in the labour market for the individual child, and acts as a further mechanism for the impoverishment of small peasant farmers, and the perpetuation of high levels of social inequality. Child labour is but another twist in the vicious circle of poverty.

Even the term 'cottage industry', in which the child works at home, should not obscure the real costs to healthy child development that it often entails. In the Indian glassware industry in Maradabad, Uttar Pradesh, nearly one-quarter of the work-force are children who work in all but one of the processes, either at home, or in workshops. Long hours, heat, gases and dust, leave many children with eye injuries and lung diseases. Working as part of a family unit is, therefore, no protection if the family is subject to exploitation, as for example within plantation labour or craft manufacture. Children working outside of their parental home on a fostering, adopted, godchild, apprenticeship basis, find themselves even more the hostages to fortune in the face of isolation and powerlessness.

To be a slave is to reach the limits of powerlessness. In India some children work for either a money lender or landowner as bonded labour to pay off the debts of parents or even grandparents. But this can easily become a contract for life: 'Sometimes, his parents or, when he grows older, he himself may take further loans, get deeper into debt and continue to work as a bonded labourer without any possibility of release.' (Blanchard, 1979, p. 55). This form of intergenerational debt resembles a feudal landlord–tenant relationship in which the child is pledged to work for the landlord or money lender, in order that a debt be paid off, or to obtain a loan or some other benefits. It continues in India despite attempts to outlaw it, most notably by the Bonded Labour System (Abolition) Act 1976. As many as 100,000 bonded labourers still exist, many of them children, and not solely in agriculture, but in such cottage style industries as brick making and match manufacture.

Child-wage labour exploitation is the easiest to document and, therefore, to campaign and legislate against. But there is ample evidence that child-wage labourers continue to work even when minimum age legislation exists. It is small-scale enterprises or 'sweatshops', often operating as subcontractors to larger enterprises, that are most adept at avoiding the usually inadequate factory inspectorate. Child-wage labour is a feature of developed and developing countries, and one which increases adult unemployment and lowers overall wages. Children are the most subordinate and cheapest form of labour, thus highly attractive to some types of employer, be they in Britain or Bangladesh. The child-wage sector can, according to Rodgers and Standing (p. 7), be analysed in terms of the following criteria: family or individual basis; method of payment – time rate or piece – share cropping system; work with a training component and without; regular or casual work and seasonal work; legal or illegal work; work compatible with schooling and work competitive with schooling. The most difficult cases to document are those in which children earn an income in the informal (marginal) non-waged sector, such as car washing, shoe shining, market trading and garbage collecting. It also includes such illegal activities as begging, petty theft and prostitution. Economists have been reluctant to analyse the informal, as opposed to the formal, sector of the economy, and yet the two are intertwined and their activities are vital to the survival of poor people, especially in urban areas. Many of these activities take place on the street, leading to the exotic phenomenon of 'street children'. This category has been notoriously difficult to define, covering as it does children who retain contact with a family and a home to those relative few who appear totally abandoned to their 'mother the street' – the true outcasts.

The sixth child activity, schooling, is vital for future participation in the adult labour force. Premature work has been shown by a host of studies to damage permanently the child's future work prospects. Not all of those children who fail to gain access to schooling, or who drop out early, enter the labour force. Many enter 'forced idleness', which is unemployment, a growing feature of some developed economies. Such a condition does not necessarily encourage the next activity, leisure, because poor children and youths find it difficult to gain access to leisure facilities or to pursue intellectually stimulating hobbies. Additionally, health activities such as adequate sleep, eating and cleaning, are difficult to maintain under the damaging work situations that have been well documented from Italy to Thailand (Valcarenghi, 1981, pp. 49–56 and Banerjee, 1980, p. 34).

The Minority Rights Group Report of 1985 suggested that it was through work that most child exploitation takes place. But when does child work become exploitative? There have been many attempts at defining exploitation in this context, however the most comprehensive formulation has been put forward by UNICEF in its 1986 Executive Board Paper (UNICEF, 1986c, pp. 3–4):

1 *Starting full-time work at too early an age*
   This happened historically in the earlier stages of industrialization in Europe where children began work in factories from nine, eight or even five years. This is still the case today in many developing countries.

2 *Working too long* within or outside of the family so that children are unable to attend school, where it is available, or to make

the most of school due to fatigue or lack of time. In some cases children still work 12–16 hours a day.

3 Work resulting in *excessive physical, social and psychological strains* upon the child as in the case of sexual exploitation in prostitution and pornography, work in sweatshops, as well as such dangerous work as military service and mining.

4 *Work and life on the streets* in unhealthy and dangerous conditions.

5 *Inadequate remuneration* for working outside of the family as in the case of child workers in carpet weaving who are paid US$3.00 for a 60-hour week.

6 *Too much responsibility too early* as in the domestic situation where children under ten may have to look after young brothers and sisters for a whole day thereby preventing school attendance.

7 *Work that does not facilitate the psychological and social development* of the child as in dull and repetitive tasks associated with industries like handicrafts.

8 *Work that inhibits the child's self-esteem* as in bonded labour and prostitution, and in a less extreme case the negative perception of 'street children'.

This framework accommodates the traditional view that the term exploitation has something to do with a third party who extracts a profit, for instance, via exploiter/employer and exploited/employee relationships. But, more importantly, it goes beyond it to embrace a 'social exploitation' dimension by acknowledging work in the informal sector (where the family can be the exploiter), as well as the human rights dimension recognizing children's subordinate position in society.

The analysis of indices of exploitation is crucial to distinguishing child work from child labour, and therefore to the setting of priorities and policies. There has been an almost universal tendency hitherto in the literature to use child work and child labour almost interchangeably as if they were synonymous. In fact, child labour is a sub-set of child work, denoting that work which is exploitative of the child. Child work becomes child labour when it threatens the health and development of children. It is child labour, and not all

Excessive strain at an early age can lead to permanent physical
damage
(*Source*: ILO)

child work, that one is trying to root out. After all, child work can be a positive experience and, in the best circumstances, children's work can prepare them for productive adult life. Through their work they can gain increasing status as family members and citizens. They can learn the skills of their parents and neighbours. Therefore, children's work can be an integral part of family life and can contribute to their healthy development. It can also build their confidence and self-esteem. Child work can then be a painless and gradual initiation into adult life.

The dividing line between socialization and exploitation will also reflect levels of development: a highly developed industrialized society, with adequate provision for the schooling of children, a full range of social services and minimum age and wage laws, will perceive exploitation of children differently from a primarily agrarian society with large numbers of rural workers and urban slum and shanty dwellers. And in practice they do. In the grey areas exploitation lives in the eye of the beholder.

Child labour has implications for the individual, the group and the wider society. It was in early industrial Britain that social investigators first associated child work with poor health. The health of exploited child workers is still being endangered today, some hundred years later. A WHO/Defence for Children (DCI) joint report on child labour states that: 'Normal growth spurts during puberty and adolescence are adversely affected by the poor nutrient intake and increased manual work' (Shah, 1985, p. 39). In 28 countries, the average per capita intake of calories is 73 to 89 per cent of what is required, but it is lower for the poorer segments of the population, from which most working children come, even though their work raises their nutritional requirements. Working children also become more susceptible to infectious diseases, including tuberculosis, if they suffer from malnutrition, anaemia, fatigue and inadequate sleep. The report cites other physical health hazards, including bone lesions and postural deformity due to working doubled-up in carpet factories and lifting heavy weights. In modern industries other health problems occur: 'The eyesight of young girls working for 12–14 hours a day in micro-computer factories is reported to be damaged within a period of 5–8 years' (Shah, 1985, p. 39). The report recognizes much work of a more rigorous scientific nature needs to be done to determine the critical age when children are prone to health hazards, the type of work and working

Table 1.1 Types of child work

Type of work	Rural	Urban
A *Within the family (unpaid)*		
1 *Domestic/household tasks*	X	X
e.g., cooking, cleaning, child-care, fetching water, cleaning utensils, washing clothes, poultry etc.		
2 *Agricultural/pastoral tasks*	X	
e.g. ploughing, weeding, harvesting, herding livestock, etc.		
3 *Handicrafts/cottage industries*	X	X
e.g., weaving, basketry, leatherwork, woodwork, household industries in the urban 'informal sector'		
B *With the family but outside the home*		
1 *Agricultural/pastoral work*		
a) migrant labour	X	
b) local agricultural labour (full-time or seasonal)	X	
2 *Domestic service*	X	X
3 *Construction work*	X	X
e.g., buildings, roads, etc.		
4 *'Informal economy'*		
e.g., laundry, recycling rubbish		
a) employed by others		X
b) self-employed		X
C *Outside the family*		
1 *Employed by others*		
a) tied/bonded/slave	X	X
b) apprentices		X
c) skilled trades	X	X
e.g., carpets, embroidery, brass and copper work		
d) industries/unskilled occupations/ mines		X
e) domestics		X
e.g., 'maids-of-all-work'		

Table 1.1 (cont.)

Type of work	Rural	Urban
f) commercial e.g., shops, restaurants		X
g) begging		X
h) prostitution and pornography		X
2 *Self-employed* informal sector work e.g., shoe-shining, car washing, recycling rubbish, running errands, selling newspapers, etc.		X

Source: UNICEF, 1986c, p. 12

environments which adversely affect health, growth and psycho-social development (Shah, 1985, p. 37).

In unregulated sweatshops occupational hazards and risks are enormous. Children often work with poorly maintained and dangerous machinery and in intrinsically dangerous work situations such as mining. Even on the streets, children can be subject to the constant threat of traffic accidents and street violence. Exploitative sweatshops often have an especially pernicious effect on children's health. Excessive noise can lead to hearing loss, and hot, damp or dusty conditions to the transmission of communicable diseases. In manufacturing, children can be exposed to toxic substances, such as glue in shoe production. Even being outdoors is not necessarily an escape as many children in modern agriculture are often exposed to lethal chemical pesticides.

Child prostitution and pornography are increasing world-wide, as is the incidence of sexually transmitted diseases. The drug trade also uses children, both as intermediaries and couriers and the children themselves often become addicted. In many cities glue-sniffing and the abuse of soft and hard drugs is endemic among street children. In developing countries large numbers of working children face the unhappy reality of increasing separation from their natural families. Poverty produces its own stress to the point that marriage and less formalized adult relationships break down. One parent or guardian leaves, or is forced to leave to find work, placing an additional burden upon the remaining single parent – often the mother – as well as the children who may be forced to work for the family's survivial. Home relationships and the economic situation may continue to deteriorate to the point where the child abandons the family, or is abandoned by it. As children's contacts with their families weaken, they lose even their limited access to basic services, such as health, education and recreation. In urban areas, children who work daily on the streets may experience a freer and more adventurous lifestyle than at home, but at the same time they encounter a much higher level of risk and less access to services and support.

Street children habitually faced with negative behaviour towards them have serious problems in maintaining healthy self-esteem and miss out on play and recreation essential for their social and emotional development. The opportunity cost of working for children is often a reduction in their chances of any kind of schooling. Formal education takes place during the day and during working hours. Therefore, a large proportion of working children do not attend school. Other constraints on regular school attendance include the cost of fees, books and uniforms as well as the often inappropriate nature of the curriculum. Meaningful apprenticeship might at least compensate for some of these disadvantages, but it can also be a form of exploitation in which the child acts as a servant to the craftsman on very low pay, running errands and performing menial tasks which bear no relation to the trade. The working child can then become locked into a vicious circle of deprivation and disadvantage in which the poor and unskilled child becomes a poor and unskilled adult.

As we have seen, children in rural areas can make an early work contribution. This, in turn, can positively influence fertility as the family views children as more hands rather than more mouths, as well as a form of social security in old age. The extent of child work in rural areas also has implications for rural emigration. As noted before, the parental use of child workers in domestic and farm activities may well allow other family members to migrate in search of seasonal or longer-term employment. Such migration usually involves male heads of households often leading to an increased work burden for the children. Conversely, lack of opportunities for child work, or a lack of adequate schooling and recreational facilities can encourage the emigration of children themselves.

Unemployment may be increased by the participation of young workers and high unemployment increases labour-force divisions. In urban industrial labour-markets, high and rising youth unemployment encourages the more affluent families to invest more in schooling, as higher qualifications are necessary to secure high-wage and high-status jobs. By contrast, among the working class, high unemployment may have the perverse effect of discouraging school attendance, not only because their labour is needed to supplement family income, but due to the perception that the amount of schooling their children could obtain would be insufficient to secure a reasonable job (Rodgers and Standing, 1981, p. 36). In fact, work experience may be more useful to them in pursuit of the job they hope to obtain. This can only perpetuate labour force divisions along class lines.

The early sexual division of labour in which boys and girls often perform different work tasks encourages a 'sexual dualism' in which men have access to non-domestic wage opportunities while women are subordinated by their relegation to domestic and subsistence farm activities. Child work can, therefore, be a mechanism by which these sex roles are learned and perpetuated. Another social outcome of child work can be seen in the commitment to a wide set of kinship obligations that the child may well carry throughout life. Child work within an extended family context is a way of socializing the child into the notion of obligations to kin which may be exploitative in nature. Child work is, thus, associated with greater inequalities of income and wealth. It is, as we have seen, both a symptom and a cause of poverty through the process of lifetime disadvantage it implies; via lack of access to schooling; through the low-wage mechanism it encourages and sustains; through the higher fertility and fragmentation of assets which it implies for the long term; or where wealthy peasant families with more children can work and therefore secure more land.

Child labour is not accidental. Many children are hired because they can be paid at much lower rates than adults. In certain industries like carpet-making or electronics assembly, children are more skilful because of the dexterity of their small fingers. But children, because of their dependent position, are the most easily exploited of all workers. They are the cheapest form of labour and their situation is analogous to that of other relatively powerless groups, such as women workers and new immigrants, who accept lower wages and poor conditions of work because of the lack of organization and their need to work. Not all child labour is therefore the result of poverty.

We have already seen the extent to which children are absorbed into the more time-intensive tasks in agrarian societies. Children are a form (perhaps the only form) of capital investment open to peasant farmers. Additionally, continuing rental obligations may force peasant families to employ all their domestic labour resources. Debt is a common mechanism that encourages this feudal-like situation and children may be the commodity traded to meet debt repayments. The growth of wage labour and capitalist relations of production has been associated in the industrialized societies with a decline in child labour in the long run. In the early stages children were used in many contexts to help further capital accumulation. It was common for whole families to be employed for a 'family wage', especially, but not exclusively, in agriculture. In developing countries today, large industrial firms and other sizeable capitalist enterprises do not seem to make extensive use of child work, perhaps because of the skill factor or the need to respect legislation, or because of the abundant supply of youth and adult workers. Nevertheless, there is one notable exception, and that is the use of child workers in small manufacturing enterprises where it is probably under-reported because of its illegality. In such enterprises children are used as cheap 'sweated' labour, frequently alongside older relatives. Such practices have been reported in both industrialized and developing countries. Here, too, child work can be a way of circumventing the potential power of trade unions as well as substituting cheap labour for higher adult wage employment.

Another correlate of capitalist relationships is the need for a wage income to pay taxes or to purchase new consumer goods, forcing many youths and children to migrate. Where farming is dominated by male workers, as in Latin America and the Caribbean, there may be a considerable amount of migration of girls and young women. Where men have been the first to move into the wage labour sector, women and children have taken over domestic and subsistence work or lower forms of wage employment, such as cotton picking and weeding (Rodgers and Standing, p. 17). Landlessness, which itself forces children into the labour-market, is another correlate of capitalist relationships. With the growth of capitalist relations the labour-market becomes increasingly differentiated and the participation of child workers can be conducive to the formation of a subordinated workers' group. Reducing the wage for subsistence permits increased exploitation. Moreover, poor access to schooling, increasingly needed in the labour-market, perpetuates disadvantage.

The situation of child workers is also affected by economic changes, such as the world-wide recession of the early 1980s. Unemployment rates rose to 51 per cent of the urban labour force in some African countries. Latin America in particular has been significantly affected by the Debt Crisis and the harsh repayment policies advocated by the International Monetary Fund turning the 1980s into the decade of debt rather than development. The effects of these trends, including increased poverty, inequitable distribution of income, and adult unemployment directly affect children. Child work in paid-wage employment outside the family has increased as children are forced to work for their own and their families' survival. This qualitative change in child work has opened up more opportunities for exploitation (ILO, 1983).

Child work is not only a response to economic processes, it also reflects the culturally determined roles and functions of children, the values by which the activities of children are judged, and the nature of the socialization process. These two sets of factors – economic and cultural – indeed go together, though the nature of the relationship has been much debated. Child labour, then, remains a seriously neglected issue in relation to the magnitude of the problem, and though the study of child labour is hampered by several particular research problems, the real constraint lies in the universal perception of it as a low-priority concern. Nevertheless, it was in industrialized societies that the problem of child labour was first identified as a public issue with attempts at systematic investigation. The prevailing view that child labour is a thing of the past needs challenging and where better to start than in the first industrial nation, Britain.

2

The Myth of Child Labour Eradication: Europe

It may seem curious to begin a regional examination of child labour with Britain. But there are cogent reasons for doing so other than those to do with convenience and national bias. Industrialization first occurred in Britain between 1780 and 1850, bringing in its wake the first widespread and impersonal exploitation of child workers. Industrialization did not invent child work; it intensified and transformed it. In reaction to the brutalities of early capitalism came the first campaigns against child labour. It was in Britain in the 1830s and 1840s that there emerged the view, perhaps for the first time, that child labour was immoral. The parallels between Victorian Britain and the contemporary developing world are striking, though one should not be tempted into drawing crude lessons.

During the classical period of industrialization, child labour was widespread, economically important and largely unquestioned morally, much as it is in the developing world today. This, of course, had long been the case. Daniel Defoe, touring the North of England in the early eighteenth century, found nothing amiss with four-year-olds at work in the domestic woollen industry. Indeed, in medieval England following the plagues of the fourteenth century, the concern had been that there would not be an adequate supply of child workers. A statute of 1388 prevented boys and girls after the age of 12 years from abandoning agricultural occupations. Children were expected to have started work before 12. After 1500, a policy was evolved of giving children training in various forms of work and crafts so that they could be self-supporting in later life. Towards the end of the sixteenth century justices were given the power to apprentice pauper childen. But the system soon came to be abused as a convenient way for parishes to absolve themselves of any responsibility for orphaned and poor children.

At the end of the eighteenth century, it was these children of the workhouses who provided the first convenient supply of labour for the new industrial textile mills. Engels talked of them being 'rented out for a number of years to the manufacturers as apprentices. They were lodged, fed, and clothed in common, and were, of course, completely the slaves of their masters, by whom they were treated with the utmost recklessness and brutality' (Engels, 1926, pp. 149–50). But soon these pauper apprentices were augmented, and then overtaken by the 'free' labour of working-class children and their parents in the new industrial cities. Nevertheless, the image of the working child as a slave became one of the most powerful psychological tools in the armoury of the early campaigners. It had first been adopted by Coleridge in 1819 when he referred to 'our poor little white slaves, the children in our cotton factories' (quoted in Cunningham, 1987, p. 6). And by the 1830s the slave analogy was at its peak, fuelling the first major investigation of child labour and subsequent reform.

The first official enquiry came with the Sadler Committee of 1832 and the Factory Commission of 1833. Both substantiate the claim that early industrial child labour was 'one of the most shameful events . . .' in British history (Thompson, 1984, p. 384). What these official investigations revealed has now passed into British folklore. Children were often employed from the age of six and made to work 14 to 16-hour days. Children were beaten awake, and kept awake by beating. At the end of the day they fell asleep, too exhausted to eat. The Commissioners could see the physical effects of this grinding and unremitting work from an early age. There was curvature of the spine and thigh bones due to protracted standing, while appalling atmospheric conditions led to chronic pulmonary complaints.

The evidence from the Commission of 1842 examining working conditions for women and children in the mines produced even more horrific stories. Boys down the pits between seven and nine years. Children lost underground and enduring 14-hour working days. The inclusion of line drawings in the report had an extraordinary effect on the Victorian public consciousness, shocked more by nakedness and the potential for sexual depravity than by anything else. The Commission of 1843 into other industries using child labour, particularly pin-pointed conditions in the pottery industry. Here, children often worked within a family unit – little consolation when they were exposed to such toxic fumes as lead and arsenic and had to work in temperatures of 100°F. Wherever the Commissioners looked in the 1830s and 1840s, despite local variations, the general picture of overwork, physical debility and gross exploitation was clear and incontrovertible. In the end, the evidence was decisive and was marshalled by campaigners whose successful outcome has been likened to a romance story (Cunningham, 1987).

The legislative changes of the early nineteenth century, which expressed a new view of childhood, had their romantic origins in the previous century with Wordsworth and Blake. Chimney sweeps were one of the first groups of working children to attract the attention of reformers at the end of the eighteenth century. However, the first pieces of legislation were applied not to chimney sweeps but to pauper apprentices. The Health and Morals of Apprentices Act of 1802 aimed to abolish night work and limit the working day in cotton mills to 12 hours. There were also provisions for schooling on Sunday and stipulations concerning proper clothing and sleeping arrangements. The 1802 Act, and the further Act of 1819 forbidding employment in cotton mills under the age of nine, were largely dead letters because of the lack of an independent inspectorate to police them.

A more significant breakthrough occurred with the Factory Act of 1833, following the evidence presented by both the Sadler Committee of 1832 and the Factory Commission of 1833. The 1833 Act set a minimum age of nine for work in textile mills. It also set maximum hours for child workers. Between the ages of nine and 13 no child was to work more than 48 hours a week, and from the age of 13 to 18 the maximum was 69 hours. Night work was outlawed for anyone under 21, but because there was no civil registration of births until the 1830s, evasion was relatively easy. Nevertheless, one important new provision was the appointment of four independent factory inspectors to police 3,000 textile establishments. Conditions were even worse in the mines as the Commission set up in 1840 revealed. The Mines Act of 1842 followed on the heels of the

Victorian child coal miners
(*Source*: ILO)

Commission's report and prohibited the employment of children under ten and women from working underground. By contrast with this initial push in the 1830s and 1840s there was little progress in the two subsequent decades. It was not until 1867 that further legislation was passed to protect children in all factories and workshops.

It was the legislation in the field of education which proved the real turning point in the Victorian campaign against child labour. The Elementary Education Act of 1870 made provision for a national system of basic education, administered through local school boards, which kept track of school attendance. The Education Act of 1880 made school attendance compulsory for the first time. Now children could only leave school at the age of ten if they satisfied attendance requirements. Those working children with poor attendance records were not allowed to leave school until they were 13. But school fees, always a constraint on school attendance, were not abolished until 1892.

However, legislation always gives an inaccurate picture of the realities of child labour, as it was never sufficient in the struggle against it. In Victorian Britain there remained many working children who were beyond the reach of these new regulations. The journalist and social researcher Henry Mayhew documented an army of street children in London. Mayhew found the number of these street children to be close to 10,000, and at the end of the century there was a growing trend for 'boy labour' in certain trades, ironically because the advent of compulsory schooling had reduced the supply of this cheaper labour. Many contemporary observers saw 'boy labour' as the cause of adult underemployment.

Legislation was also ineffective in the growing sweated trades of the East End of London which employed mostly an army of girls and women drawn to the capital in search of work. Even more invisible than the garment industry were female domestics. The 1851 census showed that more than a million women and girls were in service. By 1891 there were 1.4 million female domestics, of whom 107,167 were aged between ten and 14. For rural girls this was often the only opportunity for work. These girls were unprotected by legislation or trade unions and isolated from their family and community. Working under harsh conditions, it was little consolation to be told that this work was an ideal training for future home management. By the end of the century girls began to have more choice and many preferred to work in shops, factories and even the sweated trades, than domestic service.

Most of these girls were from the rural areas which remained largely unaffected by the new legislation. Rural child work is typically less well researched than urban industrial activities. In the rural areas children were necessary to supplement family income and to undertake the more routine tasks. Depending upon the locale and the crop, children could be found working alone, with their family, or in agricultural gangs. Harvest time put the greatest strain on families and their children. Schooling was particularly undermined. A typical school log records: 'Opened the school today, but obliged to close it for another week – harvest not finished therefore children unable to attend' (quoted in Walvin, 1982, p. 74).

Though it is difficult to compare rural working children with their urban counterparts, agricultural life was very severe, particularly within those rural-based industrial activities such as lace making, straw plaiting and glove making. Here children seemed to have the worst of all worlds. Rural activities were also much more difficult to regulate and trade unions found organizing rural workers far more difficult. The worst abuses were attacked by the Gangs Act of 1867 and the 1873 Agricultural Children's Act, forbidding the employment of children under eight and providing for their education. Yet long after 1873 it was difficult to get magistrates to convict poor parents for the non-attendance at school of their children. Gradually, compulsory education eroded this situation but part-time and casual child labour proved impossible to eradicate.

Schooling, then, and not industrial or agricultural legislation, effectively ended widespread child labour in Britain. This coincided with changes in the economy which greatly reduced the demand for child workers. To these changes was added the ideological shift in the notion of what childhood meant. In the 1830s working children were seen as 'slaves' who needed rescuing *for* freedom; by the 1840s they were viewed as 'savages' needing rescuing *from* freedom. As Cunningham points out it was only if children ceased to be either slaves or savages that they could revert to their proper dependent and protected status as children (1987, p. 8). Nevertheless, working children were a common feature of British life up until the First World War. The school leaving age was after all still 13 and work could easily be fitted around education. A survey of 1908 showed that 900,000 children worked outside of school hours. Even as late as 1905, Robert Sherod was able to publish his book entitled *The Child Slaves of Britain*. As we move into this century we see the gradual extension of the period of compulsory schooling. The Employment of Women, Children and Young Persons Act of 1920 laid down 14 as the minimum age for full-time employment in factories. The 1944 Education Act extended compulsory schooling to 15 and it was further extended to 16 in the early 1970s.

In the wake of these changes, child work has become casual and part-time, but not limited to the delivery of newspapers or occasional baby-sitting. As a reminder that not all contemporary work in Britain is of this innocent and harmless kind, the *Observer* newspaper ran a report in May 1984 of 'Slave Labour in the Rag Trade'. Earlier the *Times Educational Supplement* had run a headline: 'Call to End Child Work – National Scandal' (May 1980). Is this journalistic licence or is there still significant illegal child work in Britain today? The first problem in approaching this issue is that there is no official source of information on the employment of children for the obvious reason that it is meant not to exist. The Census of Employment is limited to adult workers and the General Household Survey draws the line at 16. Estimates of child employment have necessarily been based upon guesswork and extrapolation. According to the ILO, only 1,000 children under the age of 15 were working in the United Kingdom in 1978.

A more plausible estimate was made by the Department of Health and Social Security (DHSS) in 1975 based on the possible effects of compulsory registration of all child workers. The DHSS estimated that 750,000 registrations would be necessary for England and Wales alone in the first year of operation with 'subsequent annual numbers of at least 200,000 (quoted in MacLennan, 1985, p. 15). In June 1975 there were 2,296,300 children aged 13, 14 and 15 in England and Wales. Total estimated registrations were, therefore, nearly one-third of this population, while the annual additions imply that at least one in four children have some kind of part-time employment, other than informal jobs such as baby-sitting and running errands (MacLennan, p. 15).

In 1972 the DHSS commissioned a research project, 'Work Out of School' by Dr Emrys Davies. Dr Davies's survey took in 40 secondary schools, sampling 1,413 boys and 1,361 girls at random in the third and fourth year, representative of all children aged between 13 and 16. The aims of the research were, firstly, to reach an estimate of the extent of part-time employment among children; secondly, to gain some indication of the effectiveness of local by-laws and statutes in regulating employment; and, thirdly, to evaluate the effects of part-time work on educational attainment. Two categories of work were defined. Category A jobs were the so-called real work carried out for remuneration, while Category B jobs referred to activities which fell outside the scope of legal regulation. The levels of child work under both of these categories as revealed by Dr Davies's survey can be seen in table 2.1. Altogether, 23 per cent of girls and 42 per cent of boys were found to have part-time jobs which were covered by regulations. A breakdown of the types of job done can be

Table 2.1 Employment of children in category A and B
jobs, by sex

	Girls (%)	Boys (%)
Not employed	20	31
Employed in category A jobs only	7	24
Employed in both category A and B jobs	16	18
Employed in category B jobs only	57	27
Total employed	80	69

Source: Work out of school, *Education*, 10 November 1972

seen in table 2.2. The survey found that children were being
employed in a number of industries, most notably shop work.
Demand for child workers depended upon the economic circumstances of the local area. Resort areas, for example, provided opportunities for child work in related service industries.

Table 2.2 Types of employment under category A

	Girls (%)	Boys (%)
Delivery of newspapers and other commodities	25	62
Shop and allied work	35	14
Farm work	9	10
Catering	10	2
Manual work	10	9
Hairdressing	7	–
Unclassified	4	3

Source: Work out of school, *Education*, 10 November 1972

Category B jobs involved mostly domestic work, child care and manual work such as car washing and gardening. Girls were more involved in these activities than boys and often held more than one type of employment in this category. Overall, nearly half of all school children between the ages of 13 and 16 were found to be in paid work irrespective of whether it was covered by any regulation. Not surprisingly, the report found that those children who were most involved in work also had the least commitment to schooling and poorer educational attainment. The survey also drew attention to the ineffectiveness of legal regulation on child work. In general, regulations were ignored and the local authorities did not have the resources or in some cases the willingness to enforce them. Dr Davies concluded that steps should be taken to standardize local authority regulations and that education welfare departments should be brought up to adequate staffing levels in order that they be satisfactorily supervised and enforced.

The publication of the report in 1972 stimulated a public debate on the statutory regulation of child work which culminated in the Employment of Children Act of 1973. The Bill was introduced into Parliament by Jeffrey Archer who stated: 'There has been a demand for it in the constituencies and it is wanted by all parties. We shall be glad to see it passed into Law and on the Statute Book' (quoted in MacLennan, p. 19). Though the Act was passed it was not implemented and has remained a dead letter for practical reasons. The additional staff resources, especially of Educational Welfare Officers, in times of recession has proved impossible to secure under both Labour and Conservative administrations.

A decade after the Act, the Low Pay Unit and the Open University conducted a survey of over 1,700 school children in London, Luton and Bedfordshire which only underlined the need for a more uniform approach to the problem of illegal child work. The survey found that 40 per cent of all children were working during term time in jobs other than the usual innocent baby-sitting, etc. Children were employed in a wide variety of jobs as table 2.3 reveals.

The researchers found that 11 and 12-year olds were almost as likely to be working as older groups and that boys were generally more likely to be employed than girls. Nearly one in ten children had more than one job, and half of these had more than two. So even the high proportion of child work underestimates the use of child

Table 2.3 Children's jobs, London, Luton and Bedfordshire

Job	Boys	Girls	Total	%
Delivering newspapers	172	52	224	33.0
Milk round or other deliveries	45	7	47	6.9
Shopwork				
Newsagents or tobacconists	15	15	30	4.4
Grocery, bakery or other foods	27	14	41	6.0
Clothing or department store	7	3	10	1.5
Shoe shop	7	5	12	1.8
Other type of shop or store	11	10	21	3.1
Hairdressers	4	6	10	1.5
Launderette or drycleaners	1	4	5	7.6
Cleaning offices, hotels etc.	25	28	53	12.8
Furniture making or removals	10	1	11	1.6
Building construction, decoration or repair	40	5	45	6.6
Garage or petrol station	30	4	34	5.0
Sewing or making things to sell	4	14	18	2.6
Typing, filing or bookkeeping	1	11	12	1.8
Pub or off-licence	26	14	40	5.9
Hotel, restaurant, cafe, etc.	11	9	20	2.9
Street market or fair ground	31	11	42	6.2
Modelling, acting or dancing	7	6	13	1.9
Stable, kennel or riding school	7	36	43	6.3
Other work with animals	16	21	37	5.5
Farming	60	32	92	13.6
Miscellaneous	33	45	78	11.5
Total working	436	242	678	100.0

Source: MacLennan, 1985, p. 24.

workers. Interestingly, the survey showed that child work was not a particular feature of London life – a kind of throw-back to Dickens and Mayhew. In fact, a regional breakdown shows that children were considerably more likely to be working in rural Bedfordshire or Luton as table 2.4 shows.

School-based surveys are likely to understate the problem for one important reason. A 10 per cent absenteeism rate is normal in most secondary schools, but is usually exceeded in some inner-city areas where the rates can be around 50 per cent. One-third of these absences may be related to work commitments (Hansard, quoted in MacLennan, 1985, p. 525). The survey also found that the majority of children were working illegally, either because they were under-aged, were working illegal hours, or were working in jobs they should not have been doing. More disturbing is the evidence uncovered of health and safety regulations being ignored. Of the survey group, nearly one-third of all boys and 29 per cent of girls reported some accident or injury.

Agriculture remains an industry both inherently dangerous and one into which children can still naturally slip. The ILO report of 1983 specifically drew attention to the number of child deaths on British farms. Between 1969 and 1975, 517 people were killed on British farms. Alarmingly, 105 of these deaths were of children. By

Table 2.4 Children in the survey, London and Luton/Bedfordshire

Age	No. boys	No. girls	Total	%
11	54	40	94	6
12	178	136	314	18
13	161	156	417	15
14	289	171	460	17
15	246	127	373	22
16	27	13	40	2
All	1,055	643	1,698	100

Source: MacLennan, 1985, p. 24

1984 child fatalities were down to four, but were up again to 10 in 1985 (Landworker, 1986). Not all of these deaths occurred because children were working. Nevertheless, many farm fatalities are due to tractors overturning, which children can legally drive from the age of 13. And though the trade unions have tried to raise this minimum age to 17, the employers counter by arguing that farmer's children have been brought up on the farm and are used to handling complex equipment.

Children continue to work on a casual basis in agriculture. In parts of eastern England, farm labour is still recruited through sub-contractors called 'gangmasters'. Farmers contract out jobs like intensive vegetable cropping to gangmasters whose interest lies in employing the cheapest labour, usually that of gypsy women and children. These practices of 'lump labour' deny workers normal employment rights and clearly lead to wage exploitation. Children can legally work on farms from the age of 13. In 1985 the BBC TV programme *Brass Tacks* focused on a carrot-topping factory in East Anglia where during the evening shift, from 5 p.m. to 8 p.m., 30 per cent of the production was processed by children aged nine years and upwards, earning a piece-work rate of 70p an hour (the minimum agricultural rate for 1985 was 86p, which itself was thought inadequate). Parents approved, with some mothers putting their children on these gang labour buses after school. Though this work is illegal, these sheds are termed 'factories' and, therefore, lie outside the scope of the agricultural union. Because so many regulations exist and responsibility for enforcement is diffused, nobody is quite sure who should act. The capacity to monitor such cases has declined in Britain. There are an estimated 750 general factory inspectors in Britain to cover some 730,000 manufacturing establishments. With regular factory inspection down from every two years to every four, Britain's child labour exploiters have never had it so good. (See table 2.5.) In 1984, the ILO noted this general decline in labour inspection and the British government was asked to say what it would do to remedy the situation. The state of affairs is reflected in the declining rate of convictions for illegal child work. The main legislation covering the employment of children is the Children and Young Persons Act 1933. This limits the employment of children to those aged over 13 and under 16 years, and provides that no child may be employed before 7 a.m. or after 7 p.m. on any day, before the close of school, or for more than two hours on any

Table 2.5 Health and Safety Inspectorate – cases and
convictions of illegal child employment,
1972–81

	Employers	No. of cases	Convictions	Penalties (in £s)
1972	7	29	29	1,160
1974	26	86	79	1,496
1976	10	11	10	595
1978	11	26	25	2,055
1980	8	18	18	975
1981	4	5	5	350

Source: *Hansard*, 18 May 1977, 9 December 1982

day on which he/she is required to attend school; for more than two
hours on any Sunday, or to lift, carry or move anything so heavy as to
be likely to cause injury. The 1933 Act allowed local authorities to
pass by-laws which would further condition child employment.
They can, if they wish, allow children under 13 to do light
agricultural work with their parents or guardians. They may limit
the number of pre-school work hours to one and may prohibit
absolutely the employment of children in any occupation which
they deem unsuitable. This has led inevitably to local variations
which the 1973 Act had hoped to end. Instead, in 1976 the DHSS
circulated a set of model by-laws. By 1985 all but one local authority
(the Scilly Isles) had revised their by-laws to conform to the degree of
standardization envisaged in the 1973 Act.

What of international instruments regulating child work? The
main instrument here is the ILO Convention 138 (1973). At the
UN Seminar on Child Labour in 1985, the UK delegate set out the
reasons for British non-ratification: 'In the past it has not been
thought necessary to enact legislation in order to conform with ILO
Conventions in areas normally controlled by collective bargaining,
and in which the prevailing standards are at least as high as those
required by the Conventions.' A more specific reason given was that
it would require legislation to oblige employers to keep additional

records, which would create an extra burden and, it is felt, might deter them from employing young people (Longford, 1985, pp. 8–9). The official view is that it is unnecessary to submit periodic reports to the ILO when current practice meets the standards of the Convention. Besides, there is little point in ratifying something that cannot be implemented. This is both hypocritical and unrealistic. The UK takes the majority stance on Convention 138, and there seems no likelihood it will change it in the foreseeable future.

During the UN Seminar the USSR delegation caused some momentary embarassment by quoting out of context the findings of the 1985 Low Pay Unit Survey. This was easy for the UK delegate to counter. But the suggestion put forward in reply, that all child work in the UK was of the light part-time variety, which did not interefere with schooling, does not stand up to close examination; neither does the claim that children do not work out of economic necessity. The only issue to which the UK delegate drew attention, as giving cause for concern, was the extent of sexual exploitation.

As is typically the case with child prostitution, little hard evidence exists concerning its extent. The journalist Gitta Sereny suggests that an unknown number of the 13,000 to 15,000 juveniles who are reported as missing from home in England and Wales each year could be supporting themselves through prostitution. Added to this figure are the thousands of schoolchildren who take part in casual prostitution to meet material wants, giving a new meaning to the concept of 'target worker'. Neither do the figures include children in care who run away from children's homes and other institutions. In England and Wales this would add another 6,000 to the figures. Significantly, too, no account is taken of Scotland, and yet the majority of runaways arriving in London are Scottish, mostly girls. The Children's Society has suggested that there are 75,000 missing children in Britain today, but readily admits that there are better statistics on missing dogs. In a country where computers can log a credit card purchase in seconds, there is no central record of the children who are at home or school one moment and missing the next (*Observer*, 30 October 1988).

According to Sereny, the incidence of child prostitution has increased dramatically in England with the recession. This has increased the supply of children who turn to prostitution because of financial need. And yet there is a reluctance on the part of the authorities to recognize that the problem exists, let alone to begin to ask the question why there are so many 'rent boys' in London's West End. Ironically, it is because child work laws exist which prevent full-time employment that runaway children are more likely to be forced into prostitution for economic survial.

The charity Centrepoint, the West End emergency youth shelter, estimates that there are 50,000 16–19-year-olds without proper accommodation in London: an increase of 35 per cent since benefit changes in April 1988. A Centrepoint survey showed that one in five homeless young men and women had been approached to become involved in prostitution (*Independent*, 4 January 1988). Street children are once again a feature of the London urban scene, as a new generation of 'Artful Dodgers' haunt tube and railway stations. Children like 14-year-old Darren, who has been living on the streets for 18 months, are part of this Dickensian enclave. Begging has becomed central to these children, and what may start as expedient soon becomes a habbit. But drug-dealing, burglary, robbery and prostitution are the more extreme stratagems for survival. Following the April 1988 social security cuts, there is now no legal income for the majority of 16- and 17-year-olds who are not in work or Youth Training Schemes. Far from being hooked on a benefit culture, these children are entering the far more damaging dependency culture of the streets. There is every sign that more young people will finish up on the streets of the capital. Centrepoint predicts more cuts are likely to add to the more than 14 such changes since 1980 (*Independent*, 3 December 1988).

Even for the child who stays at home, the earnings from work may be an important contribution to family income. The Low Pay Unit/ Open University survey found that of the 67 children who were working, only 13 received any pocket money. Child earnings can be a substitution for pocket money or they can be a way of reducing the financial demands on hard-pressed parents. The relationship between children's income and family income may be indirect, either through meeting expenditure on clothes or entertainment, or by subsidizing family income by working in the family business.

The researchers were also able to examine the proportion of working children according to the socio-economic and employment status of their parents. As can be seen in table 2.6, though the sample is small and must therefore be treated with caution, there appears to be a relationship between parents' unemployment and the likelihood of child work. Where parents are unemployed or on a low income,

Table 2.6 Child labour and social class

OPCS[a]	Total	% working	No. in family business
I	0	–	–
II	13	38	4
III NM	8	25	1
III Manual	43	51	8
IV	28	36	–
V	5	20	–
Unemployed	21	52	–

[a] Office of Population Censuses and Surveys. Class I = professional etc. occupations; II = intermediate occupations; III NM = skilled occupations, non-manual; III Manual = skilled occupations, manual; IV = partly skilled occupations, manual; V = unskilled occupations, manual.
Source: MacLennan, 1985, p. 31

there may be an added incentive for their children to work. As the researchers for the BBC *Brass Tacks* programme on child work in East Anglia found: 'For a family where the dole or carrot-topping wages are the only income, a child's £8 is a significant amount of money' (quoted in Franklin, 1986, p. 140). Of course, there are those in contemporary Britain who see children working as a positive return to Victorian values, and as character-forming for these 'pint-sized entrepreneurs'. Others see in the current preoccupation with deregulation of working conditions and free-market forces a possible return to a new Victorian Age of 'pauper apprentices'.

When we look at continental Europe we can observe similar structural factors which sustain the continuation of child labour. Italy is thought to have the largest number of working children in Western Europe – perhaps as many as 1.5 million children. The worst areas are Naples, Milan, Turin, Genoa and the provinces of Apulia, Sicily and Lazio (Valcarenghi, 1981). Southern Italy, in particular, shares many characteristics with the developing world. The south is relatively economically backward and still highly dependent upon agriculture. Children are in this context expected to contribute to family income. Some of the social relationships still appear feudal, as in the case of markets where farmers hire a boy for the whole agricultural year. Such was the experience of Michele Colonna, who was sold at the age of 11 in the market square of Altamura. After four years of grinding work as a shepherd, he committed suicide in November 1976. Public opinion was temporarily outraged. But today, travelling in southern Italy and Sardinia, you can still see little shepherd boys, like Michele, roaming the mountain slopes from dawn to dusk with their flocks.

Valcarenghi, in her report for the Anti-Slavery Society (1981), suggested that three major interlocking factors were in play in sustaining the high incidence of child work in Italy. Firstly, there is the factor of poverty. Most people know about the south, but there are also deprived areas in the regions of Friuli, Venetia and Sardinia. Even in the relatively affluent north there are pockets of poverty in Milan, Turin and Genoa, which are augmented by the continuous migration from south to north and from rural areas to the urban centres. The lower rate of child work in the poorer regions of Abruzzi and Molise is more a reflection of the fewer opportunities for child work. The necessity for children to contribute to the family income is not, however, the only reason. Parents see work as a better alternative to hanging around on the street. The street is often the only alternative for the poor child when home consists of one room which must accommodate six or more people. There is also the rationalization from parents that at work the child may be learning a task, and thereby improving their prospects for full-time work when at the age of 14 or 15 they can work legally. Besides, there is the deeply ingrained view that a child is the parents' property. For families of peasant origin the state has no right to tell them how to treat their children or to fine them when they fail to send them to school.

A major factor in the causal chain after economic and family circumstances is the changing nature of the productive structure. Demand for child workers has increased in recent years due to the decentralization of production now taking place in Italy. This takes the form of a widely scattered number of artisan-type workshops. Some of these are not registered. They offer opportunities for illegal work and, as a result, employ children. These workshops are not in the main autonomous, but depend on larger enterprises, which in turn may be dependent upon others, all the way to a large corporation at the top. FIAT, the state-run car giant, uses this sytem of decentralized production. Many motor car accessories are commissioned from outside firms and spread among a wide range of small production units. This also happens, to take another example, in the footwear industry where a small workshop will make shoes for a larger firm, while at the same time producing a small quantity for local sale.

This system of vertical integration encourages the use of child workers and has a number of advantages, including: tax avoidance; reduction of overheads, evasion of national insurance obligations; payment of wages on a piece-rate basis; evasion of responsibility for occupational diseases; accidents at work or pollution of the environment; freedom to engage and dismiss workers and to alter working hours to suit production needs; and immunity from trade union power and strikes. Children who find themselves in these workshops are at the bottom of the decentralized ladder, trapped in low pay and unhealthy and unsafe working conditions.

Finally, the State and its institutions fail in their responsibilities. Schooling is deficient, the organization of leisure hours after school is left entirely in the family's hands, and the court and labour inspectorate is ineffective. Compulsory schooling in Italy is very selective and not tolerant of individual backwardness. A deficient curriculum, organization and functioning of the school system is widely viewed as a major cause of child work in Italy. Not surprisingly, this class-based system produces a high rate of truancy of around 9.4 per cent nationwide, rising to 12 per cent in the south. Besides, the state system of education in Italy, apart from a few experimental schools, consists of only four hours teaching in the morning; filling the rest of the day is entirely up to the individual. In the huge dormitory suburbs of industrial cities, in the workers' quarters in the old centres of southern towns, in the semi-deserted countryside devoid of infrastructure, children are left to spend their free time in the street or in overcrowded dwellings.

The legislative framework also appears bankrupt in the face of the inadequacy of labour inspection. In Naples the rate of truancy is 64 per cent, rendering the provincial inspectorate incapable of coping with the problem of child protection. In Milan, where there are an estimated 55,000 child workers, the labour division magistrates confess that they handle only two cases of illegal child work a week. Clearly, the problem is not that laws do not exist, but that little attempt is made to ensure their enforcement, and that conditions exist which continue to encourage the supply and demand for child workers. Child labour law is itself a relatively recent feature in Italy. The use of child workers had been recognized under a law passed by the fascist administration in 1934. The Italian Parliament tackled the issue of child work for the first time in November 1961 with the passing of Law 1325, whereby the statutory minimum age for legal employment was raised from 13 to 15. A subsequent decree issued by the President of the Republic – No. 272 of March 1964 – laid down a number of exceptions, in that it sanctioned specific types of work for children between these ages. These exceptions soon became established practice leading to further legislation in the Protection of Children and Adolescents in respect of Labour Law of 1957. This law introduced compulsory medical checks to test the fitness of children for work and periodic tests up to the age of 18 and, in some cases, up to 21. It also prohibited night work for those under 18 except those helping their family, working at home, employed aboard ships and in public organizations. Nine years later, Presidential Decree No. 432 prohibited the employment of males under 16 and females under 18 in 'tiring, dangerous and insalubrious' work. A decree of January 1971 had laid down a number of occupations involving light work in which children could be employed. Italy is also a signatory to ILO Convention 138.

At the theoretical level, Italian legislation seems to be adequate, but in terms of implementation it often appears to be a dead letter. One of the reasons for this is the conspiracy of silence which forms a bond between family and employer who share a common interest. Even when accidents occur at work, parents and employers prefer a cover-up if at all possible, settling the matter privately through financial compensation. Sometimes it is impossible to cover up accidents. In June 1975 three 14-year-old girls were burnt alive in a jeans factory in Naples while doing overtime on their own. The factory had been built illegally and its emergency doors had been bricked up out of fear of burglars. In the same year there were a number of examples of 14- and 15-year-old boys being electrocuted working alongside concrete mixers in building yards.

Milan, in the prosperous north, provides an insight into the processes outlined above. Child work had been on the increase since 1971 due to changes towards decentralized production which has transformed the area into a swarming mass of tiny offices and workshops. But the extent of child work is well concealed and one has to use indirect data from school absenteeism (55,000 children miss the morning roll call every year in the province) to gain an indication of the problem. It is concealed too by the importation of a Mafia-type system into the labour-market. Part of that system is the adherence to *omerta* or silence. Valcarenghi was only able to obtain names of children working on the understanding that the results would only be publicized abroad (p. 33). This type of production structure is easy to penetrate. For example a small firm needs a loan in order to buy a car. The loan is offered by someone with Mafia connections who then forces the employer to take on illegal child workers. Child work is not only increasing but also moving away from the traditional tertiary and other service sectors towards industry. Valcarenghi found that the average age of children working was 12, but that the majority had been working at least a year at primary school-leaving age. The average working week was five and a half days with a seven-and-a-half hour working day. These children, though born in the city, were of southern origin and most of them contributed to the family budget.

The Italian Trades Union Confederation estimates that 100,000 children work in the Naples region alone. This is hardly surprising when one realizes that it is one of the poorest areas in Western Europe. Child work is widespread, open and accepted as a fact of life. Poverty seems the main reason why children work. A survey in 1977 found that children's earnings were often an essential contribution to the family budget, especially in the case of large families dependent upon casual and irregular work. Of the 463 working children interviewed, 31 per cent contributed the whole of their earnings to their families, 74 per cent gave half and the remainder kept only their tips (quoted in Valcarenghi, p. 37). Over a third of the children said their fathers worked irregularly and a further third stated that their fathers were low-paid manual workers. The vast majority left school because they needed to work. But there is also the parental pressure which views schooling as unimportant. The average age of starting work is between ten and 14; 45 per cent leave before the final year of primary school. The school authorities, by turning a blind eye to the problem and dismissing truants as failures, encourage this high drop-out rate. For these children work becomes a way of gaining respect and a means of attaining socially approved material goals. The forms of child work were wide ranging. Over 40 per cent described themselves as errand boys, others as apprentices, carpenters, glass-makers and shop-assistants. Nearly all those not attending school were working a six-day week and a six-hour day, and the rates of pay were around one-third of those of adult workers without the usual benefits of insurance, paid holidays and pension rights.

The leather industry has been particularly singled out as an area of concern. In the leather industry, work takes place in small, badly ventilated rooms. Conditions are particularly bad in the old centre of Naples, where workshops are found in basements and garages. In such unventilated conditions toxic fumes are not dispersed. This scattered and unorganized workforce has no trade unions to fight for better health and safety measures. All the workers face the unacknowledged disease of Italy's leather trade, glue polyneuritis, which can lead to the paralysis of the upper and lower limbs. The shoe and leather industry is scattered throughout the various districts of Naples and fragmented according to the nature of the tasks undertaken in the various workshops. Firms employing fewer than 20 workers constitute a high percentage of firms in the leather industry. The main characteristics of such firms are a low level of technology, the absence of complete stages of manufacture, and the use of semi-skilled workers and outworkers. Often the boss works alongside his employees, who are almost always illegal labour and often his relatives. Neither they, nor the factory, are registered. There is no insurance cover or pension fund. The workers are paid on a piece-work basis and the number of days is dictated by the production needs of the workshop. Often the workers are ignorant of their part in the system of decentralized production. Such conditions breed exploitation and children represent the final link in the chain of exploitation.

Spain is another member of the European Community which exhibits relatively high levels of child work. A number of organizations have made estimates of the extent of children working illegally in Spain. In 1977 the Catholic Youth Workers claimed that there were more than 200,000 under 14 illegally at work, but an unstated number aged 14–16 were also illegally working, bringing the total to 1.5 million. In 1979 the socialist trade union UGT (General

Workers' Union) estimated that between 150,000 and 200,000 children under 14 were at work illegally. In addition to these estimates, official school statistics for 1978 showed that some 700,000 children of primary school age were not in fact attending school; many of these it can be stated will be working, if only casually. However, officially the number of working children as a proportion of the labour force has been declining. Official census returns suggest that in 1970 children under 15 accounted for one worker in every hundred. By 1976, this figure had dramatically dropped to less than one worker in a thousand. But, of course, official labour statistics only account for the formal economy whereas much of the illegal child work occurs in the informal unregistered sector.

Legislation to ameliorate the conditions of working children began in Spain 1855. From that date the age at which children can begin work has steadily increased. The 1944 Work Contract Law stated that children of both sexes may not undertake any form of work before their fourteenth birthday, except in agriculture, family workshops or, in determined circumstances, in public afternoon performances of a charitable nature. Agricultural work was, in any event, limited by a previous decree of 1934 to out-of-school hours. Article 134 of the Work Contract Law stated that an apprenticeship contract could not be undertaken by anyone within the compulsory age of education (ten up to 14). All child workers between 14 and 18 were the object of unions' protective legislation. But despite the 1944 Act, it was found necessary to forbid the employment of children under 14 as domestic servants. This prohibition also applied to those under 16 who had not obtained their certificate of primary studies.

On the international front, it was not until 1972 that Spain ratified the revised ILO Convention 60 of 1937, forbidding the employment in non-industrial work of children under 15 or those over 15 still undergoing compulsory primary education. In 1978 Spain ratified the ILO Convention 138 (1973) which is the most comprehensive international instrument in the field, fixing the minimum age for admission to employment at 15, with the exception of light work outside school hours and vocational training schemes. Nevertheless, the recent trend in both the labour field and education is to make the minimum age for admission to work as 16.

The Anti-Slavery Society report of 1979 (Searight) suggested that most working children were to be found in a family setting. This is the case in under-developed regions such as Andalucia and Galicia, but it is also found in well-developed northern provinces such as Navarre and Cantabria. Agriculture is still a large sector of the economy where children can be employed in almost all year round harvesting: olives in February, potatoes from April, soft fruit from May to August, grapes from July to the end of January, tomatoes from October to January. Harvesting is particularly important for Andalucians, who not only help harvest local produce, but of whom more than 30,000 emigrate each year for the grape harvest in France. The poorer families inevitably take their children which means that many children are absent from school for months on end. In Granada, Searight reported the observation that such children regularly lost two months schooling each year as a result of being away harvesting grapes in France (p. 18). Poor families from other provinces, like Valencia, are similarly involved, taking their children of seven and eight to work with them. Again, the area most open to the abuse of child workers is the sub-contracting system. This is a widespread practice in the shoe industry around Valencia, Alicante and in Majorca, and in the garment industry in Madrid and Seville. Here the factory owner pays for the work done without any obligations. The small groups which provide the finished products work how and where they like, often in private houses, and often composed of children.

Other forms of work accounting for a large number of young children are activities such as street-selling, shoe-cleaning, begging and various forms of collecting. Child beggars are considered a real problem in many parts of Spain. While begging may not be considered formally as a job, it does fall within the important economic area of the informal sector which, as we shall see later, is of considerable significance in developing countries. It is also a full-time economic activity for many Spanish children. In the summer of 1979, a Seville social worker reported to Searight that a 'plague' of woman beggars had infested the city the previous Easter, the majority with small children who were not their own. In June it was still possible to see professional child beggars in the city, despite official attempts at repelling the invasion. Some children wore a placard saying 'I am an orphan' or 'I come from a very poor family, please help'. It seems that begging is a pleasanter and more rewarding life than schooling. In the summer of 1986, I visited Seville and was able to see an extensive poster campaign on the issue of child beggars. Clearly, the problem has not gone away, though a member of the Spanish Committee for UNICEF asserted that most of these child beggars were not local gypsies (who preferred to do a real job in return for money), but immigrants from Portugal (private conversation, 1986). The problem is extensive and not just confined to the poorer south. In 1977, a special Anti-Begging Squad picked up more than 700 children in Madrid, of whom four were working alone. The UGT considered that these children represented cases of real parental exploitation, since they were beaten if they did not bring back a certain sum. Indeed the UGT claim that children are being hired to beg and being controlled by adults in a Mafia-like way (Searight, p. 22).

Another informal work activity is the collection of cardboard, old rags, foul refuse and other miscellaneous items. Members of poor families, including children in the marginal zones of Seville, Granada and Badajoz, for example, go out daily with their barrows and collect old boxes for re-sale, and food refuse for their own hens or pigs or for sale to small suburban farms. *La busca* (the search) can occupy even six-year-olds who rummage through the dustbins for any saleable object. Even being at school is not necessarily an escape from hard work in the evenings or weekends. Children work in the fields, in cafés, restaurants and streets, selling. This part-time work is particularly evident during the tourist season. Searight found widespread misgivings about the apprenticeship system as a form of cheap labour. Employers sometimes renege on their responsibilities regarding training and health and safety regulations.

Schooling, the obvious alternative to work, is often deficient. Taking Andalucia again, many primary schools in Seville are so crowded that children attend on a rota system. In such circumstances work absorbs the time left over from school. School attendance is patchy throughout Spain. A study published in 1979 showed that in Cadiz only 30 per cent of primary school pupils completed this basic stage of education, compared to the national figure of 51 per cent. Even completing primary school is no guarantee of moving on to the next stage. In 1976–7, 871 children leaving primary school in Pamplona and its zone could not find a place in secondary school, despite having the necessary qualifications. Poverty and traditional attitudes to schooling still send many children into premature working lives. Children are still removed by parents from vocational training schools run by religious bodies which meet the cost of tuition. Families, often under-educated, prefer a small immediate gain from their children rather than the expectation of higher wages after vocational training.

Both Italy and Spain share one other characteristic: they are home to a significant gypsy population within which child work is traditionally accepted and valued. An examination of child work among Europe's gypsies (their correct though less familiar name is *Roma*) is a means of bridging the gulf between East and West and exploring social marginality as a factor in child work participation. As table 2.7 shows there are six million gypsies in Europe today – more than the population of Denmark or Scotland. They remain victims of rejection and racism in almost every country. The largest communities are in the socialist countries of south-east Europe where an exceptionally high birth-rate will increase their total by an estimated 30 per cent by the end of this decade.

In the life of gypsies everything revolves around the extended family group. Gypsies, instead of being employed, often base their economy, except for seasonal work, on self-employment in small businesses with groups of men, women and children working according to their own roles. The economic activities of gypsies are extremely varied and highly variable – metal work, scrap dealing, horse dealing, entertainment and circus activities, agricultural work and begging. Socialization into these economic roles occurs at an early age. Children are encouraged to work with their parents and are given real responsibilities, for instance commerical dealing for boys and domestic work for girls. From the age of 12 onwards, children make an important economic contribution to the family unit on a footing of equality between children and adults.

Education beyond primary school is largely non-existent (barely 1 per cent in the Federal Republic of Germany) and it is generally assumed that over one-half of gypsy children of school age in Europe are not attending school. Of those who attend, many receive inappropriate instruction and are viewed by the school system as pathological. The illiteracy rates among those over the school leaving age varies between 65 and 95 per cent.

Spain illustrates many of the problems facing gypsy children in Western Europe. In Spain barely half of them receive an education and they are as likely to be working as studying. Up to 70 per cent of gypsies are thought to be illiterate and only 1.2 per cent have completed primary school (*Guardian*, 19 July 1986). About two-thirds live from scavenging for waste paper and scrap metal, street

Table 2.7 Romani population in Europe, 1985

	Romani population ('000s)	Country population ('000s)	% of Romani in country population
Yugoslavia	850	22,800	3.73
Romania	760	22,683	3.35
Spain	745	38,435	1.95
Hungary	560	10,700	5.21
Turkey	545	50,207	1.09
USSR	530	275,000	0.19
Bulgaria	475	8,969	5.3
Czechoslovakia	410	15,400	2.66
France	260	54,872	0.47
Greece	140	9,984	1.4
Italy	120	56,556	0.21
Portugal	105	10,045	1.05
UK	90	56,023	0.16
West Germany	84	61,387	0.14
Albania	80	2,906	2.75
Poland	70	36,887	0.19
Netherlands	40	14,437	0.28
Switzerland	35	6,477	0.54
Belgium	20	10,000	0.2
Austria	19	7,579	0.01
Ireland	18	3,375	0.53
Sweden	15	8,335	0.18
Finland	8	4,873	0.16
Norway	5	4,145	0.12
Denmark	4.5	5,100	0.09
East Germany	2.5	16,718	0.01
Total	5,991	813,893	0.74

Based on available census figures and previous estimates (taking into account high birth-rate) and including associated sedentary and nomadic groups.

Source: Puxton, 1987, p. 13

trading and seasonal work. Gypsy children always work in a family setting. It is against the gypsy ethos to allow children to do paid work in workshops or areas outside the family group. Schooling is a particular problem, even though only 10 per cent of gypsies are nomads. Popular prejudice holds that gypsies do not want their children to go to school, but others argue that the system itself prevents this. Because they live in shanty towns, most gypsies cannot produce the residency document needed to register their children in school. Even when special efforts are made to circumvent this problem, prejudice reappears. In February 1986 police had to be called in to control crowds of angry parents protesting at the admission of gypsy children to a Madrid school. So, ironically, despite the gypsy contribution to an image of Spain which helps to sustain a $8,000 million a year tourist industry, the gypsies are a despised minority. Even the tourist industry exploits gypsy children, as with the case I witnessed of a nine-year-old flamenco dancer in Granada who was working in a club despite her mother's protests to the owner that they were both being worked too hard.

Another marginal group are the estimated 150,000 tinkers concentrated in Old Castile, Extremadura and the Ebro valley. Their traditional occupation used to be travelling the country, selling and repairing metal household goods. With rural migration, better communications and the arrival of plastic, they lost their rural customers and their livelihood. Migrating to the towns, they have found it hard to find jobs. Almost 90 per cent of the adult population is illiterate. Family solidarity is strong among tinkers and they prefer to isolate themselves from the rest of the community. Few of their children go to school and the authorities apparently make little attempt to integrate them into the educational system. It can be assumed that many of these children are working in one way or another.

Yugoslavia has the largest gypsy population in Europe and through emigration has important links with countries in Western Europe and even the United States (where there are an estimated one million gypsies) and Australia. It was not until 1981 that gypsies were given the same minority status as the Serbs, Croats, and Slovenes. And since 1983 the Romani language has been introduced into the school system. Even so, most gypsies live below the average standard of living, especially in the developed northern regions where they have become shanty dwellers and their children illegal workers. It was from such areas that an organized trade in child slave thieves was exposed in 1986.

Gypsy children working in organized gangs for latter-day Fagins are suspected of operating in Spain and Greece, but have definitely been found in Austria, Germany, Switzerland and France. However, the centre of this operation is Italy, where the vast majority of the child slave thieves are Yugoslav gypsies. The children usually cross the international frontier hidden in lorries and in the boots of cars, and once in Italy they are taken to bleak camps on the outskirts of the big cities, principally Milan and Turin. The most notorious is Milan's gypsy site, Campo Muggiano. After training in bag snatching, pickpocketing and burglary, the children are sold a second time, this time to the criminal gangs. The children are used cynically to exploit the Italian penal code. As long as the child is under 14 there can be no prosecution, even if the child is illegally earning four to five hundred pounds a day. The Belgrade newspaper *Politika* estimated that 10,000 children had been sold across the frontier with Italy in the decade up to 1985, and that in that year the price for a trained child varied from £2,500 to £3,000. In 1984, just over 1,000 Yugoslav children were returned from Italy, but many will simply be sent back. The Yugoslav police have identified five main towns, Skopje, Ljubljana, Rijeka, Pula and Zagreb, which are used as collecting centres for these child thieves.

As in Latin America where the poorer families allow their children to be 'adopted' by the rich, so Yugoslav gypsies part with a child to a 'benefactor' in order to have one less mouth to feed. It was when a group of gypsy boys walked into a Milan police station in March 1986, frightened, crying and suffering from malnutrition, that the Italian authorities were alerted to the magnitude of this trade in gypsy child slaves. In the trials which followed in October 1986 and March 1987, Italian legal history was made when Yugoslav traffickers and controllers were prosecuted under national and international instruments proscribing slavery – including the Geneva Convention. This allowed the Italian authorities to impose heavier penalties than would normally be the case.

Yugoslavia has adopted a relatively enlightened policy towards gypsies, recognizing their nationality, which has begun to influence other socialist states. The norm has tended to be assimilation and a forced end to travelling, as in the USSR where nomadism has been outlawed for 30 years. The socialist states may start from the theoretical premise that it is the duty of the state to assist underdeveloped groups – the practice can be otherwise. When I visited Romania in the summer of 1986 there was little attempt to disguise official hostility towards gypsies who make up one of the largest national minorities. Many still travel but suffer harrassment by the police and are unable to send their children to school. Clearly their children work illegally, as must be the case in Czechoslovakia where only one child in six completes the upper grades in elementary school. By the end of the century there will be over six million gypsies in the socialist states. Bulgaria, Romania, Hungary and Czechoslovakia all contain gypsy minorities approaching 5 per cent or more of the population. Given their high birth-rate the number of economically active children must be significant. In the face of the ideological stance of the socialist states and the absence of hard data, the welfare of gypsy children provides one seed of doubt that child labour has been consigned to the scrap heap of history in Eastern Europe.

Finally, on 17 May 1989 the European Commission unveiled its draft social charter. One of the 12 'fundamental social rights' listed is concerned with the prevention of child labour. A stark reminder that even in the wealthiest societies, child labour continues to defy attempts to eliminate it.

3

The Myth of Child Labour Eradication: The USA

Colonial America reflected the prevailing values of English society. English immigrants to America in the seventeenth century soon passed laws putting children to work, especially in the production of textiles. An order-in-council in New York of 1710 provided for 30 children between three and 15 years old to be apprenticed. Even the diary of George Washington describes a duck-cloth factory in Boston where, 'each spinner has a small girl to turn the wheel and where the whipping of these factory children was commonplace' (Challis and Elliman, 1979, p. 64). From the beginning of European settlement in America there was a labour shortage. As most men were engaged in clearing the land and farming, women and children were the only people free to do manufacturing work. During the Revolutionary period, when supplies from England were cut off, manufacturing grew and so did the demand for child workers.

When the industrial revolution came to America it produced the same qualitative change in child work as in Britain. Testimony in a Massachusetts Bureau of Labour Report suggests that conditions in the cotton mills were every bit as bad as those in Britain:

> We run our mills sixty-six hours per week. When I began as a boy in the mill, I worked fifteen hours a day. I used to go in at a quarter past four in the morning and work until a quarter to eight at night, having thirty minutes for breakfast and the same for dinner, drinking tea after ringing out at night. But I took breakfast and dinner at the mill as the time was too short to go

home, so that I was sixteen hour in the mill. This I did for eleven years, 1837–1848. (Quoted in Cole, 1980, p. 203)

The employment of children in manufacturing continued to increase in the nineteenth century with the opening up of new markets in the West and even greater shortages of men for factory work.

In the United States people first became concerned about child work because it did not leave time for reading. Puritans, in particular, believed a person came into clearest contact with God through reading the Bible. Many people also believed that democracy was founded on a literate citizenry. This led the Connecticut legislature to pass a law in 1813 requiring factory children to be taught basic literacy and numeracy. Massachusetts, Rhode Island and Pennsylvania passed similar laws.

In the period just before the Civil War, several northern states passed laws prohibiting children under a certain age from working in factories, mills and mines. A law passed by Massachusetts in 1836 required factory children to have at least three months' education in the preceding year. And the first attempts at reducing the working hours for children were aimed at allowing them some time for education. By 1863 seven states had passed laws limiting the hours of child workers, but in Massachusetts this only applied to children under 12 and in Connecticut only to those under 14. In 1848 Pennsylvania became the first state to outlaw the employment of young children when it passed a law prohibiting the employment of children under 12 in cotton, woollen, silk or flax factories. This minimum age was raised to 13 a year later, when the law was extended to the paper and bagging industries, but unlike Britain there was no system of inspection. Though several northern states followed the example of Pennsylvania, children in the southern states continued to be widely employed during and after the Civil War, some as young as six or seven years old would work a 13-hour day (Challis and Elliman, 1979, p. 64). Indeed the 1900 census showed that 1,750,178 children aged between ten and 15 were employed, an increase over one million compared to the preceding 30 years.

The period from 1880–1914 has been characterized as the 'child saving era' (Platt, 1969). This reflected a changing perception of children, who were seen as having 'the right to childhood'. It was also an era when large numbers of immigrants inhabited the growing urban areas and where slums, poverty, crime and ethnic ghettos seemed to threaten the established social order. Small bands of street children roamed the towns and cities, sometimes stealing and breaking windows. Other children worked as street vendors, artists and factory workers. Such developments alarmed the reformers who emerged from the upper and middle classes with a new view of children's rights. Education became a child's right; through it the child could be redeemed. Child labour was seen as impairing the health and development of children and depriving the child of the right to play. Education would keep children off the streets and out of the factories, as well as prepare them for an occupation. It was during the great economic depression from 1893 to 1896 that the campaign against child labour really developed as part of the Progressive Movement. As in Britain half a century earlier, the reformers investigated conditions in order to mobilize public sentiment. These investigations into factories, mines, home working, street trades and agriculture, were publicized in popular magazines.

The first organized campaigns took place in the South. Alabama's Child Labor Committee founded by Edgar Murphy, an Episcopal clergyman, was the first such organization in the USA. Murphy himself took the photographs to expose child labour in textile mills which appeared in the Committee's most effective publication, *Pictures from the Mills*. In 1903 a minimum age of 12 years and a maximum working week of 66 hours was passed. And in 1902–3 15 states passed child labour laws. During this period, as a result of these states campaigning, a National Child Labor Committee was established, which held its first meeting on 15 April 1904. One of the first issues the Committee decided to focus on was the 10,000 illegal child miners in the Pennsylvania coal fields. Many of these children were employed picking out slate and waste from coal as it passed along chutes, over which they were suspended on wooden boards. This working position was not simply backbreaking but highly dangerous. Should a boy slip into the coal he had little chance of surviving intact. The Committee's investigators found it difficult to uncover the facts due to the pressure on the boys to conceal the truth. Nevertheless, the Committee finally succeeded in getting a new law passed in Pennsylvania in 1909. By this time child work was at its height, but the Committee had 5,000 members and was rapidly

A Pennsylvania coal miner
(*Source*: ILO)

expanding its activities and moving into new areas such as the glass-making industry. At the turn of the century some two-thirds of the 7,000 boys under 16 years employed in America's glass factories were kept at work overnight, at least every other week. Up to 98 per cent of them worked in the intense heat of the furnace rooms. The night shift was from 5 p.m. to 3 a.m. Mortality figures were high. Again, the Committee used photographic evidence, and the first breakthrough was in New Jersey, which established a minimum age of 16 for night work in 1910. Indiana, Pennsylvania and West Viriginia soon followed suit. Photographs taken by the now famous Lewis W. Hine were used to counter the claims of textile mill-owners in the south that the conditions were better there than in other forms of employment. But the classic conditions in the mills for child workers took their customary toll. A federal report of 1910 described children only 50 inches tall and emaciated, but working a 12 hour day.

The Committee at this time decided that the most effective counter to child labour was federal legislation. The campaign for federal laws was particularly stimulated by conditions in the south where manufacturing had expanded rapidly during the last two decades of the nineteenth century with a consequent demand for cheap labour. Most southern states refused to regulate child work as it provided them with a competitive advantage. After a long and difficult campaign, the first federal law regulating work of those under 18 was passed by the United States Congress in 1916. In 1918 the Keating–Owen Act was declared unconstitutional by the Supreme Court. It proved difficult to pass child labour laws because many groups within the society did not wish to have them. Many arguments were put forward which have a universal ring to them: they would interfere with the rights of parents; they would deny poor parents the economic support of their children; children had a right to work and it was good for them; without child work American industry would be uncompetitive in world markets. As in Britain almost a century before, child work was itself in decline at the stage when it became subjected to systematic attack. This was due to changes in the economy and a new awareness of the value of education. By 1933 most states had laws requiring school attendance up to 14 years of age. In 1938 Congress passed the Fair Labor Standards Act which has provided the legislative framework until today. The major provisions of the FLSA are as follows:

Occupations *except* in agriculture:
— 16-year minimum age applies to all non-agricultural employment *except*,
    — employment is permitted by regulation or order of the Secretary of Labor in occupations outside of mining or manufacturing if this employment is deemed to not constitute oppressive child labour and is confined to periods that will not interfere with their schooling or overall health or well-being,
— 18-year minimum age in any occupations declared hazardous by the Secretary of Labor,
— the Act exempts the employment of children by their own parents except in hazardous occupations declared by the Secretary of Labor or in manufacturing or mining.

Occupations in agriculture:
— 16-year age minimum for work in agriculture during school hours and in hazardous occupations,
— 14-year age minimum for work in agriculture outside school hours,
— 12–13-year age minimum with written parental consent,
— under 12 years of age on farms owned or operated by the child's parents or on farms in which all employees are exempt from the minimum wage provisions of the FLSA.

Typically, the extent of child work was already significantly in decline by this time as table 3.1 reveals.

By 1950, previously excluded areas of employment that were brought within FLSA had been incorporated and the US Bureau of the Census discontinued publishing data on workers less than 16 years of age.

Today 14 is the lower limit to obtain a work permit and this has become in effect the legal minimum age. There is no minimum age for modelling or performing. These require special work permits. In New York and other states, newspaper carriers have to be at least 12 years old and have a special work permit. In other states no permit is needed and the minimum age for delivering papers is as low as ten. When there is a conflict between the federal and state child labour laws, the regulation which is the stricter standard must be followed.

Table 3.1 Child labour in the USA, 1880–1930

Year	Children 10–15	All occupations	Non-agriculture	All occupations (%)	Non-agriculture (%)
1880	6,649,483	1,118,356	396,504	16.8	6.0
1890	8,322,373	1,503,771	591,568	18.1	7.1
1900	9,613,252	1,750,178	686,213	18.2	7.1
1910	10,828,365	1,990,225	557,797	18.4	5.2
1920	12,502,582	1,060,858	413,549	8.5	3.3
1930	14,300,576	667,118	197,621	4.7	1.4

Source: Revd Vincent A. McQuade, 1938, *The American Catholic Attitude on Child Labour since 1891*, Catholic University of America, Washington DC, p. 9

Federal regulations prohibit work for under-16s during the hours school is in session and between 7 p.m. and 7 a.m. During the school year work is limited to a maximum of three hours a day and 18 hours a week. During school vacations children can work as late as 9 p.m. and as many as eight hours a day – 40 hours a week. Everyone whose work is covered by the Fair Labor Standards Act must be paid according to the minimum wage provisions of the Act, no matter how old they are. States can set higher rates and all businesses, then, have to comply with the higher rate. The belief in 1950, which exists to this day in the USA, is that child labour is insignificant. As the US representative at the UN Seminar on Child Labour stated, '. . . the exploitation of children working in the United States is no longer a major social or political problem' (Berrington, 1985, p. 9). There-fore, the current official view is that 'child labour exploitation . . . is not considered a major policy problem in the United States today' (Berrington, p. 7). Nevertheless, the US representative did concede that there was concern over migrants and refugee families, and in agriculture and the garment industry. In particular, the delegate pointed to the employment of 10–11-year olds in agriculture which uses chemicals to control pests and weeds as a difficult 'policy problem'. In a good natured riposte, the observer who worked with the United Farm Workers exposed the extent to which the official view was being economical with the truth.

UN seminars are not perhaps the place for disarming candour. What the delegate failed to spell out was the extent of the failure to make much impact on child work in agriculture. The much quoted statistic of 800,000 children working on farms and plantations throughout the USA goes back to 1971 but was repeated at the Seminar and comes from the United States Civil Rights Commission 1978. Children are 25 per cent of the paid labour force in agriculture and predictably it is the children of immigrant families who are the most exploited. A study covering 12 states found that in seven of them most migrant children worked illegally, often leaving school by the age of 12 to work full-time (Challis and Elliman, 1979, pp. 69–70).

In the early 1970s a Quaker group called the American Friends Service Committee (AFSC) surveyed the extent of child work in the agricultural industries of Washington, Oregon, Ohio, Maine and California. In Washington, the AFSC estimated that 99 per cent of all migrant children over the age of six worked in fields during the picking season from June to September when temperatures ranged between 90° and 100°F. In Oregon it was estimated that 75 per cent of the seasonal force were children. In Ohio, 30,000 migrants moved into the state each year to pick sugar beet and cucumbers, many of them small children. In both Maine and California the use of chemicals added to the health hazards, especially in California, where 25 per cent of the state's 400,000 farm workers were children (Challis and Elliman, 1979, pp. 70–1).

What this evidence shows is the almost universal exception of agriculture from child labour regulations, where it is often thought to be a special case, and the difficulties of developing trade unionism within the industry. In the US, as elsewhere, child labour in agriculture is part of the more general problem of adult workers who receive lower wages and protection than workers in other industries. The campaign against child labour on the farm is therefore one element in a much wider fight for union recognition. This is best exemplified in the so-called 'Blue Sky Sweatshops' of California's farm industry and of the long struggle of César Chávez's United Farm Workers (UFW), founded in 1962.

In 1968, Peter Matthiessen was able to describe the following scene, as a group of strikers watched the non-union workers:

Down the rows the 'campesinos' squatted under the low vines. Grape workers pick and pack in teams, ordinarily the team is a family group, and some of the children in the fields are no more than eight years old. . . . Like the rest of California's commendable labor legislation, the child labor laws are not enforced expect under duress, and enforcement, in this case, would be resisted by workers, who expect the children to help out. 'We have accepted child labour.' Chávez said, 'because otherwise our families couldn't survive.' But the 'helping out' is not restricted to light work, the younger the worker, the more skilled he is apt to be at cutting and packing, so that the heavy labor of lugging grapes often falls upon the youngest children. (Challis and Elliman, 1979, p. 73)

In 1974 Chávez changed his policy and announced that his union aimed to eliminate child labour from the fields of California. Over a decade later the union was still appealing for support in its campaign against child labour:

Child abuse is getting a lot of attention. But child labour – a form of child abuse – is still common in California, Arizona, Texas and throughout the nation. Some 800,000 underaged children survive by harvesting crops with their families across America. Malnutrition among migrant kids is 10 times higher than the national rate, farm workers' babies suffer 25% higher infant mortality and some are born deformed because of toxic pesticides carelessly sprayed in the fields. Kids as young as six years old have voted in state-conducted union elections since they qualified as workers. 'Without them we couldn't survive,' one migrant parent admitted. Many growers say children are in the fields because their parents want them to work. Some well-meaning people think the answer is better education and more social programs. We disagree! Where farm workers enjoy the protection of UFW contracts we have succeeded in nearly eliminating this vile abuse. These workers earn enough so they don't have to migrate anymore with their children, their kids go to school and they can afford to live in decent homes instead of rancid farm labour camps. But only about 20% of California farm workers enjoy these protections; for the rest, poverty and

The 'Wrath of Grapes' campaign sticker
(*Source*: United Farm Workers)

abuse are daily facts of life. We in the UFW are working to change that. (*Food and Justice*, Vol. 2, No. 2, 1985)

If the fight against child labour is, as the UFW claims, bound-up with union recognition then it is ironic that the National Labor Relations Act, which is the primary law in the US protecting the rights of workers to organize, specifically excludes agricultural workers. Only two states, California and Arizona, have their own pieces of protective legislation. As the counsel for the UFW at the UN Seminar declared: 'Our experience indicates that there is going to be no headway made in protecting children from exploitation in the fields, unless there is specific legislation, on a national level, that protects all the migrant workers, all the farm workers, in every state, with a strong and uniform application of the law' (Lloyd, 1985, p. 3).

Indeed the claim was made that the Reagan administration appeared to be dismantling the National Labor Relations Board, which administrates the National Labor Relations Act, rendering it less effective as a body for protecting workers' rights. Though California was the first state to adopt an Agricultural Labor Relations Act, the union claims it has been rendered useless by the administration's attitude of non-enforcement. Violation of state labour laws constitutes a misdemeanour with a maximum punishment of six months jail and/or a fine of US$200 (1979).

There are no mandatory health checks for adult or child workers in agriculture. This is critical where workers use pesticides. The UFW counsel particularly argued for a 'zero-risk factor' in the use of pesticides by child workers, a suggestion which would create panic among growers in California. Yet this would be a clear way of creating an economic disincentive for hiring child workers. 'By adopting the position that any grower, any agricultural corporation, any huge agri-business, anyone who wants to have more than a zero-risk factor in the fields in terms of pesticides, or workplaces in terms of chemical subtances, can do so, but cannot have children in those fields, or in those workplaces' (Lloyd, 1985, p. 10). It was a point which eventually registered with the UN Seminar with Recommendation (d), that States should arrange for research into the effects on children of exposure to pesticides and other dangerous substances (UN, 1986, p. 26). Recommendation (p) could also be seen as of relevance to the US: 'Particular priority should be given to the eradication of the most abhorrent forms of child exploitation, in particular prostitution and employment in hazardous activities.'

It was the omission of any reference to child prostitution that was the most striking feature of the US presentation at the Seminar, since Dr Judianne Densens-Gerber, before the House of Representatives, in 1977 quoted a figure of one million child prostitutes in the US. In testimony before the Committee on the Judiciary United States Senate, in November 1981, Ernest Allen, stated that child pornography and prostitution was '. . . indeed a national epidemic' (Allen, 1981). Others, like Daniel Campagna, see child prostitution in the US as a vast and lucrative industry whose income even exceeds the gross national product of many developing countries (Campagna, 1985, p. 15).

Ennew has questioned both estimates and talks of the 'exaggeration effect' (Ennew, 1986a). The figure of one million child prostitutes is a guesstimate based on extrapolating from the estimate of 300,000 boy prostitutes found in the research of Robin Lloyd. Dr Densens-Gerber assumed that there would be more girl prostitutes and so added 600,000 to this figure without adding any independent evidence. But then Lloyd used subjective assessments as he admits: 'In the early stages of research for this book I approached police officers and leaders of the gay community with a working figure of 300,000 boy prostitutes in the United States alone. Deputy District Attorney James Grodin in Los Angeles said, "You won't get any argument from this office for that figure." During a television interview I offered the same figure to Morris Knight, the West Coast gay activist. Said Knight, "It might well be double that amount."' But equally it might be considerably less and one must keep in mind that Lloyd was constructing a piece of popular journalism which feeds a popular imagination conditioned by films such as *Taxi Driver* in which Jodie Foster played a New York child prostitute.

Equally, Daniel Campagna's 'Meat Rack' report may also be in the sensational/exaggeration mode. His report took three years and collected information from 596 police departments in 50 states, augmented by a survey of 125 social service agencies and field studies in selected cities. His estimate of the gross revenue from child prostitution in the US is based upon a very simple formula using a 'conservative' estimate of US$15 per transaction and a set of variables concerning maximum and minimum working day to provide the information in table 3.2:

Campagna's conclusions are as follows:

> These figures are, to say the least, both enlightening and astonishing in their implications. The gross annual revenue varies from almost 2 billion to 78 million dollars, depending on the volume of the juvenile prostitutes selected for cross-

Table 3.2 The economics of child prostitution in the USA

$V \times A \times B = R\ (\$000)$			
Base number of prostitutes (V)	Working days (A)	Daily income (B)	Annual gross revenue (R)
200,000	208/104[a]	$45/15[b]	1,872,000/312,000
150,000	208/104	$45/15	1,404,000/234,000
100,000	208/104	$45/15	936,000/156,000
50,000	208/104	$45/15	468,000/78,000

[a] Estimated at maximum 4 or minimum 2 working days a week × 52 weeks.
[b] Estimated at maximum 3 or minimum 1 transaction(s) a day × $15.
Source: Campagna, 1985, p. 15

indexing. Even at the lowest level (50,000 prostitutes corresponding to just 50% of the minimum estimated figure), the income is at least equal to, if not greater than, the gross national product of many developing nations. Keeping in mind that this table uses extremely conservative base figures for the A and B variables, the results clearly indicate that, in addition to being sexually used, child prostitutes are economically active on a systematic, unprecedented scale in the United States (Campagna, 1985, p. 15).

Ennew has pointed to a number of methodological problems which should caution one against the author's undoubted ingenuity. The figure of $15 per transaction was taken from police and social workers and not from either the children or clients. As we shall see later, children often prostitute themselves for small sums, or petty items in a casual way. The assumed frequency rate for transaction can be attacked for similar imprecision. Added to this is his exaggeration regarding developing countries. There are none with a GNP of less than two million dollars. And nowhere does he present evidence that the trade he describes is systematic (Ennew, 1986a, pp. 78–9).

Comparative data seems to contradict Campagna's claim that we are witnessing child prostitution on an unprecedented scale. Following the campaigning work in England of William Stead (there were an estimated 100,000 child prostitutes in Victorian London), reformers in the US took up the cause of child prostitution which produced, 'a nation-wide panic that reached its height during the years 1911–15. In the quiet of their homes, middle-class families devoured journalistic accounts of the ruin of young women in the hands of sinister procurers armed with poisoned needles and drugged drinks. Young girls, the headlines screamed, were being sold into virtual sexual slavery' (Rosen, 1982, p. 112). Finally, posters appeared in conspicuous places in major urban areas with the warning: 'Danger! Mothers beware! Sixty thousand innocent girls wanted to take the place of sixty thousand white slaves who will die this year in the United States' (Rosen, 1982, p. 115).

On the supply side of child prostitution in the US and Europe there are some indications of a connection between certain forms of family life and child prostitution. Studies in the US suggest that many children become involved in prostitution after they have run away from home. Lloyd's estimate of 300,000 boy prostitutes designates most of them as runaways. And Sereny quotes an annual figure of between 750,000 and one million runaways in the US as being generally accepted (Sereny, 1984, p. xiii).

In a study based on 12 years of research in child prostitution and pornography in the US, Janus and Heid Bracey (1980) identified three broad groups of children who leave home:

Runaways, who persistently and determinedly leave home.
Walkaways, who come and go from their homes.
Throwaways, who are rejected or whose absence is of little or no consequence to their parents.

Their research also suggested that the majority of children involved in prostitution come from households with one or more of the following characteristics:

Non-nuclear family structure (73 per cent).
Parental drug abuse (26 per cent).
Parental alcohol abuse (60 per cent).
Sexual abuse in the home (64 per cent).

But again, methodological problems arise in the use of small samples with no control group. One can only note at this stage that there may be a causal relationship involved in the factors above. Moreover, a Canadian Government survey of 229 juvenile prostitutes in eight cities states: 'These youths came from families in all walks of life while some had been sexually abused as children; their experience in this regard was no different from that of other Canadian children' (1984).

In Seattle in the 1980s there were 600–800 street children living off drugs and prostitution. They may be 'streetwise' but they are missing out on childhood, in the richest society on earth. What hope, then, of eradicating child labour elsewhere, if it persists so tenaciously in the richest society on earth? We must now turn our attention to developing countries where most child labour is found today. And for the sake of convenience we can divide the next two chapters into rural and urban contexts.

4

Child Labour in Developing Countries: The Rural Sector

It is important to begin with the rural sector in developing countries because it accounts for the majority of child work in the world today. In reality, the rural and urban sectors in developing countries are closely interrelated, with a high degree of mobility of labour (including child labour) between them. Many of the industries in which the most excessive abuses of children's work are found are located in rural areas (mines and quarries, carpet-weaving, match factories, etc.) and draw their labour force from the small-peasant, near-landless and landless households of rural areas. It is because most child soldiers are taken from the rural areas that I have included an analysis of this issue as part of this chapter.

There is the common view that child work in rural areas is unproblematic because it is within a family context. 'Children assist their families . . . at the home from early years on, they also assist in farms, shops, etc. But this is not what we call child labour. Rather, we have in mind work in employment situations where children are engaged on a more or less regular basis to earn a livelihood for themselves or their families' (Bequele, 1986, p. 11). Such an assumption was echoed at the UN Seminar in 1985. The representatives of Bangladesh, Ivory Coast, Colombia, Egypt, Algeria and Syria, among others, regarded child work within the family as a duty or honour and an expression of family solidarity. We should be sceptical of such ingrained assumptions. Many children make a deliberate choice in favour of 'exploitation outside the home' and control of their own earnings, often in the face of parental opposition,

rather than endure the 'eternal apprenticeship' of long hours without remuneration under the control of parents. Not only is it true that many millions of poor families have no choice but to demand long hours of work from their children, there is also some trade-off between the burdens of parental and child work. This parental power, as the ASS suggests, can be more absolute than that of an employer or the state (1984, p. 46). The issue of parental power is the most sensitive area in the child labour field and the most difficult for outsiders to tackle. Parents can reduce their own work burdens through the use of their chidren's work.

All five categories of child work (domestic; non-domestic; non-monetary; tied or bonded labour; wage labour; marginal economic activities) are represented in the rural sectors in developing countries. The major difference between the urban and rural sectors is probably the low frequency of 'marginal' activities in the rural areas. There can be no easy assumption that the more 'primitive' the rural society the more likely one is to encounter child labour. In most hunting and gathering societies, and many societies practising shifting cultivation, time allocation studies have shown a remarkably low incidence of child work. These societies are ones in which the labour demands on adults are not great compared with peasant societies practising settled agriculture. Among pastoral nomads, there appears to be a wide variation in overall levels of work inputs and therefore of child work. Often, these are considerably lower than those in settled agricultural peasant societies in the same region. Many studies of peasant societies agree that children are viewed as sources of labour, to be put to work at an early age, and that the demand for children's labour is positively related to the relatively high rates of fertility, which characterize many peasant societies.

High work inputs of children are found in frontier societies with relative land abundance and in other situations where labour rather than land is the main constraint in increasing agricultural production. Kamuzora's study in Bukoba district, Tanzania, shows boys and girls both in the 5–9 and 10–19 age category working in domestic and in direct economic tasks, about one-half those of

Girl harvesting in Indonesia
(*Source*: ILO)

adults. The work inputs of children in the 10–19 age group were not much different from those of younger children, mainly because these older children were also spending about five hours daily in school. For these older children the total hours of 'work plus school' amounted to almost nine hours per day, i.e. more than the total daily work time of adults (quoted in White, 1985, pp. 6–7).

Not so immediately obvious is that the demand for child work is also high in the very densely populated rural societies of Asia, often thought to be characterized by massive labour surplus and underemployment (like Tara in Bangladesh, where average farm sizes are now in the region of 0.5 hectares). These conditions force households into very long hours of work for a very low return, in a wide variety of activities outside the family farm (including working for wages on others' farms, petty trading, handicrafts, etc.). In such situations several studies have shown the relative economic advantage which accrues to parents with relatively large families (e.g. Cain, 1977; White, 1976). White found in the village of Kali Loro in Java, Indonesia, that one-half of all working hours among near-landless and landless households were contributed by children (White, 1985, p. 7).

The tenacity of marginal peasant households to hang on to a tiny plot of land and resist, or at least postpone, complete dispossession and proletarization is often explained by what Chayanov (1925) called 'self-exploitation'. But it should be stressed, as White does, that the child's actual work contribution is determined by the parents' ability to control the labour of the child. Many authors, therefore, take care to describe the rigid and authoritarian patriarchal relations between the generations in the wider society. Self-exploitation is not a completely accurate description of the situation, since it is more a case of the rigid control of the labour of subordinate family members, through relations of gender and age hierarchy, by the male household head (White, 1985, p. 7).

It is these marginal peasant households who have historically provided the source of labour for large-scale capitalist farming and corporate agri-business concerns. It appears that the majority of these enterprises, generally producing export crops, make widespread use of underpaid child workers alongside adults. Recruitment mechanisms vary, but such labour is usually hired on a casual rather than a permanent basis. Long hours make school attendance impossible and they can, of course, be disposed of with ease when no longer required. Though the qualitative aspect of exploitation of non-domestic child work has been described as more damaging in the urban, industrial context, household labour in the rural context can be just as exploitative and detrimental to child development. This is the case where the child is part of an exploited household unit, or exploited within the household by parents who stand *in loco parentis* (ASS, 1984b, p. 45).

Child workers who are caught up in the slave-like system of bonded labour are viewed as a priority concern in the child labour field. Debt bondage is a form of modern slavery and recognized as such by the United Nations. India is generally acknowledged to represent the worst case of this, despite successive legislative attempts to abolish it. The current definition of debt bondage was formulated by the United Nations Supplementary Convention on the Abolition of Slavery, the Slave Trade and Institutions and Practices similar to Slavery, in 1956. The Convention states: 'Debt bondage, that is to say, the status or condition arising from a pledge by a debtor of his personal services or those of a person under his control as security for a debt; if the value of the services as reasonably assessed, is not applied towards the liquidation of the debt or the length and nature of, those services are not respectively limited and defined.' As one might expect, this insidious type of slavery is particularly difficult to identify in practice as it takes many forms and has so many different local names, some of which are intended to hide what is both exploitative and illegal. Many of the contracts are individual and unique.

Debt slaves were a well-known phenomenon in earlier civilizations, such as ancient Athens. This form of slavery can be contrasted with chattel slavery in which the slave is not paid for his/her labour and can be regarded as an instrument of production. In the case of debt bondage, a tenant or debtor voluntarily places himself/herself in a servile position, even though there may be little choice in the matter. Bonded labour is not, theoretically, the exclusive property of the master. The bonded labourer is a technically free wage or share-cropper whose state of servitude may be terminated on payment of the debt.

In contemporary India, where conservative estimates of bonded labourers start at 3 million, debt bondage is the condition of a person, who needing to raise a loan and having no security to offer, pledges his/her labour, or that of someone under his/her control, as a security for the loan. In some cases the interest on the loan is so high that it cannot be paid; in others, the labour given is deemed to repay the interest on the loan but not the capital. Thus, the loan is inherited and perpetuated. It becomes a contract for life and a form of inter-generational debt and slavery. Children can, and are, pledged as part of this system. The caste system reinforces and perpetuates debt bondage. The landlords or money lenders are of a higher caste than those who seek the loans, who are generally harijan (the untouchables) or adivasis (tribal people outside the caste system and regarded as beneath it).

Bonded labour persists, in part, because of the considerable sums of money needed even by the poor to celebrate weddings and festivals or to repay government loans. There is, therefore, a considerable recourse to the extensive network of money lenders. Advances of food, grain or cash may also be made to rural peasant farmers or landless labourers to see them over an off-season. Illiteracy and innumeracy help money lenders to enmesh bonded labourers. In the unlikely event of a contract existing they can neither read the agreement nor calculate the current balance or rate of interest, thus allowing the debt to continue through the generations. Children become a commodity in this process. Parents have an absolute power over their children, which makes it possible for children to be pledged chattel-like to pay off debts.

The system endures despite legal attempts to abolish it. In India some acts of prohibition date as early as 1915 (The Abolition of Jeeta Services), while an act specifically mentioning children (The Children (Pledging of Labour) Act) was passed in 1933 with amendments in 1950 and 1951. In 1976 all forms of bonded labour were abolished by the Bonded Labour System (Abolition) Act. Nevertheless, the chairman and founder of the Delhi-based Bonded Liberation Front (BLF) has testified that there are between 80 and 100 million bonded labourers in India, many of them children. In what has been called a historical judgement, Justice Bhaguati of the Supreme Court of India made a judgement on debt bondage as a result of BLF pressure to investigate the condition of quarry workers in Faridabad. The court concluded that all people working for less than the legal minimum wage must be considered bonded labourers (Whittaker, 1985, p. 72).

According to the Anti-Slavery Society, in the district around the holy city of Benares about 100,000 children are working in the carpet industry. In common with other children labouring in bondage, some have been kidnapped and virtually sold, while others have taken the place of relatives (Whittaker, 1985, p. 73). In another case, children, many under 14, were among 100 labourers found by a judge of the Supreme Court of India locked up at night in a cage. They were discovered in the Utter Pradesh village of Joshiyara where they were in bondage to the Continental Construction Company. The judge reported that the men and boys had been bonded with the full knowledge of the labour inspectors who connived with the company (*Daily Telegraph*, 4 October 1985). Such cases lend weight to Swami Agnivesh's claim: 'The government makes laws for the poor and keeps them in a library.' In Faridabad, only 10 miles from the Supreme Court, there are at least 10,000 bonded labourers (Whittaker, 1985, p. 74). Though bonded labour is most widespread in rural areas among agricultural workers, 6 to 11 per cent of whom may be caught up in the system (ASS, 1984b, p. 22), there are reports of child bonded labourers in the service industries, for instance as teaboys in Calcutta. Manufacturing industries also operate with bonded labour, especially in family cottage-type industries as, for example in brick making (*Times of India*, 1981) and the match industry of Sivakasi (Mitra, 1984).

Egalitarian land reforms and the provision of adequate credit facilities for those of poor credit risk would help undermine the system. Standing suggests that because the system does not directly benefit monopoly national or international capital, the state may be susceptible to reformist pressures if effectively exposed by social scientists and trade unions (Standing, 1982, p. 615). In other words, bonded labour ought to be singled out for priority targeting by child labour campaigners because it expresses an extreme form of exploitation, is common, and may be less well defended.

The large corporate plantations, on the other hand, do come under the national and international capital category. They employ tens of thousands of workers in Assam, Sri Lanka, Malaysia and North Sumatra, and have their own resident labour force descended from indentured labourers recruited during the colonial period from peasant populations, usually from other countries. Though minimum wage regulations usually exist, with stipulations that plantations provide children with education, it appears to be still part of the corporate labour strategy to maintain the isolated 'enclave' conditions of the work-force and to limit access to education and mobility. Trade unions have sometimes been active in pressing for better conditions for adult permanent workers, but they have generally not taken up the cause of casual workers, including children. Children are found working in the fields and processing, and also in domestic duties to free their mothers to work. The working hours are often at least seven hours a day and their wages, when paid at all, are usually half that of adult men. The work can be dangerous, as for instance when highly toxic pesticides and weed killers are used without protective clothing.

Jomo et al.'s study of Malaysian plantations (INSAN, 1984) underscores many of these general features. The use of casual labour in the estate sector is quite persistent where the majority of the population is from south India, mainly Tamils. Though children are not directly employed, their labour is solicited insidiously through the contract system. Various forms of work, ranging from pesticide spraying, picking cocoa pods, and weeding, to stacking oil palm fronds are given out to contractors on a piece-rate basis. Not infrequently, contractors employ children who provide cheap labour. Management can then plead that they are not responsible for child workers as they have not employed them directly.

Children in the rubber estates perform various activities for which they are not paid because they are part of the family, which functions as a single economic unit. Parents burdened with heavy workloads and for whom minimum wages depend on tapping at least 500 trees or harvesting 150 to 200 bunches (or 2 tonnes) of oil palm have no choice but to have their children help them. Jomo's survey showed that 56 per cent of working children in the rubber estates were between 10 and 12, while in the oil palm plantations 60 per cent of child workers were in the 6–10 age group.

Schooling is rarely an alternative for these children; of the 1,766 rubber estates in Malaysia, only 335 (19 per cent) provided schooling, while only 16 per cent of oil palm estates provided schooling (Jomo et al., 1984, p. 23). The plantation workers' children generally receive their primary schooling in the estate Tamil schools. Poor facilities, limited teachers and the parental indifference towards schooling (29 per cent of parents had never attended school) all conspire to lock the already disadvantaged Tamil pupils into educational disadvantage and fatalism. Recent reports have found that 78 per cent of estate children drop out of primary school while only 0.4 per cent of children complete secondary education where the medium of instruction is the Malay language.

There is little or no institutional protection for estate children from the Labour Department, trade unions and political parties. Though children work on the estates, there are no records at the Ministry of Labour of child labour on plantations. This can in part be attributed to weak enforcement and monitoring of labour laws by the Ministry as there are only 198 Labour Officers in the country for more than three million wage earners. Jomo has also criticized the National Union of Plantation Workers (NUPW), the only trade union representing plantation workers, for playing a paternalistic role towards its members while collaborating with the government, plantation owners and the other vested interests. According to Jomo, it has avoided mobilizing estate workers, preferring to let the government protect the NUPW's exclusive status in the face of grassroot frustration and agitation as well as efforts to organize outside the NUPW. The NUPW does not have records of child labour in the estates: 'It has remained largely silent on the issue of child labour on plantations, apparently preferring to "play safe" by turning a blind eye to the glaring existence of the problem' (Jomo, 1984, p. 28).

The fact that the majority of plantation workers are Hindu Tamils, and, therefore, belong to a small ethnic and religious minority, has also meant that there is little official incentive to be concerned with the conditions of plantation labour. In any event there are no laws in Malaysia which explicitly forbid children from working. Finally, unless forced to do so, there is little reason to expect the estate management to alleviate the conditions, par-ticularly the piece-rate system, which contributes to the incidence of child labour on plantations.

In this case a hope for improvement might be thought possible because of the large scale and relative visibility of plantations and the activities of various pressure groups (however half-hearted). However, plantations which see their profits threatened by welfare developments can easily find ways to place their work-force beyond the reach of regulations. The use of casual workers and contract labour (as in Malaysia) on piece-work rather than time rates, with a minimum daily work target beyond the capacity of a single adult does, as we have seen, compel the use of children who never appear in the labour statistics.

In countering such strategies, the ASS has recommended '. . . that both national and international trade unions be encouraged to treat the question of minimum wages for adult plantation workers as a priority, this should be combined with demands for better education and communication with the wider society, in order to end social isolation.' (1984c, p. 4). Traditionally, and by legal necessity in many cases, estates are obliged to provide health and social amenities for workers. This means that the enclave nature is maintained, as the wider community does not have to bear the cost. In the event, the amenities often are not provided, since they are beyond the means of all but the most prosperous estates. The ASS recommends that this legislative situation should cease and in the words of the ILO Committee on Work on Plantations: 'all these social services have to be provided to the community as a whole and not just to one category of workers.' (quoted in ASS, 1984c, p. 5).

In many parts of the developing world one can observe a trend away from the giant estate or plantation towards the so-called 'out-grower' or 'smallholder nucleus estate' farm. Under such schemes, which are often supported by international development agencies, the plantation is replaced by a number of smallholder 'family' farms of approximately equal size, who undertake the direct field production of the crops while the 'nucleus' (which may be a state or private company) provides the necessary inputs and extension, some supervision, and purchases the unprocessed crop. Unlike the plantation, the 'nucleus' is not involved in wage relations but only in market relations with the producers, and can thus neatly shift all the problems of labour control on to the smallholder household. The consequences of this development for child workers turns on one's view of whether helping on the family farm is an expression of 'family solidarity' as compared with their direct exploitation through a wage-employment relationship. The last people who will be asked for their views are the children themselves, who will work much as before, but without any direct remuneration or control over the product of their labour.

Agro-processing industries using child and juvenile labour have adopted modes of labour recruitment and control which parallel the well-known conditions of the 'runaway' electronics industries in free-trade zones (White, 1985). A good example is that provided by Arizpet Aranda (1981) of the Mexican strawberry industry, a highly seasonal business serving the US market in the winter months. In the small town of Zarmora, strawberry cleaning and packing plants are able to recruit as many as 10,000 young, generally unmarried women, from the surrounding peasant villages, and then to release them when they are no longer required. Girls, who generally begin this work at 12–15 years of age, are eager to leave the confines of the peasant household, and are therefore willing to accept the abrupt fluctuations in employment and the low wages which go with them. Because none of them plan to work in the plants for more than a few years, they are less likely to organize and demand improvements in hiring and working conditions.

In a different context the move to the new 'production responsibility' systems in the People's Republic of China, in which the production of food and other crops is no longer undertaken by production brigades or teams but by individual peasant households, appears to have put a premium on child workers. With this return to the 'peasant family', many households appear to have made decisions not to comply with the 'one-child family' policy. Additionally, there is evidence of recent declines in primary and middle school rolls; peasant girls in particular have been withdrawn from full-time education in order to earn incomes (Croll, 1984). The authorities now admit to a significant child labour problem in the rural areas.

To shift the regional focus once more, children are particularly vulnerable to exploitation under a regime of aparthied. The ASS report on South Africa (1983) gave indications of the possible extent of child labour in agriculture using casual/contract systems of recruitment. Agriculture in South Africa is the country's largest employer of black labour, including child workers. Casual workers form 43 per cent of the total agricultural labour force, and are employed for the seasonal, labour intensive work required in producing fruit, vegetables, sugar, wheat and in sheep shearing. Many casual workers appear to be women and children from the Bantustans. In the fruit and wine-producing areas of Western Cape, farmers simply drive into the outskirts of Cape Town in trucks and pick up workers. These are predominantly from street gangs, turning the usual cycle of migration into full circle (ASS, p. 41).

The ASS found labour pools, for example in the district of Sekhukhuneland in Lebowa Bantustan, which supplied cheap black labour to white farms in the Eastern Transvaal. According to representatives in the district, 'almost anyone who requires cheap labour comes here to pick up young girls. They pick up anyone from ten years and upwards to do anything, from agricultural weeding to harvesting' (ASS, p. 28). These children are often misled about the nature of the work expected of them. It is the farm's practice to register as few of them as possible, so that they are subject to the insecurities of illegal workers. They are paid below subsistence wages and live in squalid conditions. If they are registered it is impossible for them to leave because their identity documents are removed on registration, and without these they can find no other work and go nowhere else in the country. If they are not registered, more often than not they are forced to remain and work as the alternative is starvation. Even past Ministers of Agriculture in the Republic have used child labour on their own farms. It is hard not to agree that the examples exposed by the ASS and the media over the years are tantamount in some cases to slave labour.

For those who approach child labour from the children's rights angle, child soldiers have become a growing cause for concern in recent years. Defence for Children International, founded during the International Year of the Child, now views the participation of children in military action as a dangerous form of work under ILO Convention 138 (*International Children's Rights Monitor*, 1985/2.2). Children's participation in military service is, of course, hardly a modern phenomenon. In England there is the account of Abbot Aelfric writing in AD 1020: 'The township was ordered to equip two soldiers for the army. Then two boy foundlings brought up in the village were chosen for that military service' (Hayes, 1985). In modern times a conscript of 1813 from France looked back over the campaign against the Russians and Prussians, and recalled 'from all sides, by small woods, over the hedges, through the gardens, our soldiers entered and turned about to fire. They came from all the regiments, without caps, and with uniforms torn, covered with blood, looking furious . . . they were all children, real children, out of fifteen or twenty not a single one had a moustache, but courage is born into the Frenchman.' (Erckmann-Chatrian, 1864). In this century there is the evocative example of Jack Cornwell, enlisting in the British Navy while still not 16 years of age, and being killed at the battle of Jutland six months later. A few days after his death he had become a hero, decorated with the Victoria Cross, and his picture was prominently displayed in 12,000 schools all over Britain, as a powerful recruitment device (Ennew, 1985b, pp. 18–19). In the

Second World War one of the last pictures of Adolf Hitler shows him congratulating adolescent soldiers recruited in a desperate attempt to defend the Third Reich.

Since 1945, the United Nations Department for Disarmament Affairs estimates that there have been 150 armed conflicts. Practically all of these have taken place in Africa, Asia and Latin America. In 1988 armed conflict was taking place in 40 countries in the developing world. Children are not the only victims of these conflicts, as part of the high civilian casualties, but are increasingly recruited by paramilitary and guerrilla forces as combatants. According to UNICEF (1986b, p. 16), this alarming trend appears to be growing in many conflict zones of Africa, Asia and Latin America. Human rights groups in Latin America have accused the authorities of breaking national conscription laws, while anti-government guerrillas are also known to have kidnapped teenagers. In 25 countries, young men are eligible to go to war at an earlier age than they are eligible to vote. In the same report, UNICEF suggested that there were 20 countries in which children from 10–18 years, sometimes younger, were involved in military training and informal activities linked with various civil wars, armies of liberation and even international war (UNICEF, 1986b, 16–17).

The international community has been very slow in adjusting to the fact that children can be active participants in war. International conventions on the protection of children in warfare are remarkably conservative on the subject of child soldiers. As most agreements regarding children are based on their protection, it is not surprising that the international community seems reluctant to admit that a child can also be a killer (Ennew, 1985b, p. 19). In particular there seems to be a contradiction in the international community's thinking on childhood in that the Geneva Conventions and Protocols seem to regard childhood as ending earlier in situations of armed conflict than the ILO, for instance, considers it does at the workplace. Article 77 of the Protocols added in 1977 to the 1949 Geneva Conventions states that:

2. The Parties to the conflict shall take all feasible measures in order that children who have not obtained the age of 15 years do not take a direct part in hostilities and, in particular, they should refrain from recruiting them into armed forces. In recruiting among those persons who have attained the age of

15 years but who have not attained the age of 18 years, the
Parties to the conflict shall endeavour to give priority to those
who are oldest.

However, there are limitations on the legal basis of the international humanitarian laws. The Diplomatic Conference, which
met in Geneva between 1974 and 1977, and the two additional
Protocols failed to improve the implementation mechanism in
situations of international armed conflict. There is no protecting
power, no optional commission of enquiry and no role for the
United Nations in Protocol II (Veuthey, 1983 in UNICEF, 1986b,
p. 15). By June 1985, 61 states had signed and ratified the four
conventions.

Under ILO Convention 138, the minimum age for full-time
employment is set at 15, but Article 3 states: 'The minimum age for
admission to any type of employment or work which by its nature in
the circumstances in which it is carried out is likely to jeopardise the
health, safety or morals of young persons, shall not be less than 18
years.' While Recommendation 146 adds: 'Where the minimum age
for admission to types of employment or work which are likely to
jeopardise the health, safety or morals of young persons is still below
18 years, immediate steps shall be taken to raise it to that level.'

Nevertheless, as Ennew points out, '. . . neither the ILO nor any
other organisation concerned with child labour seems to regard
child soldiers as endangered child workers, despite the fact that most
people would agree with Ruskin's comment that "the soldier's trade,
verily and essentially, is not slaying but being slain!"' (Ennew,
1985b, p. 19). In fact, soon after this case was made that soldiering
should be seen not as serving but as hazardous work, DCI took the
point up at the UN Seminar. This case for the inclusion of child
soldiers in the list of priority concerns relating to child labour was
supported by the NGOs, during the Seminar and featured in the set
of conclusions: 'The exploitation of child labour takes many forms,
and certain types of exploitation, for example, child prostitution and
the employment of children in hazardous occupations including
armed conflict, are particularly abhorrent.'

The current realities pay little attention to these international
ideals. The Iran/Iraq war (1980–8) has given most concern in recent
years. An Iranian government spokesman said on 6 May 1982
'children have taken part in the frontline ever since the first days of

the war, and we are proud of them.' Durng the first two years of the war an estimated 50,000 Iranian child soldiers died in the south-west of Iran. A number of accounts reveal the strength of the various pressures on families and children to participate in the war. In an interview reported in *Der Spiegel* (No. 23, 1984), Ayatollah Khomeini spoke of the sale of (Iranian) children and their fate as mercenaries in the Gulf War. He stated that sometimes boys of poor parents went to the front to help their families financially. *L'Express* (25 March 1983) suggested that if the child died the parents received a cash sum and a martyr's card which gave them the right to reduced prices for certain goods and priority in the labour market. The Martyr Fund, supported by the State Treasury, national enterprises and private donations grew to a considerable size (*Guardian*, 16 March 1984). Mme Iranclokhte's statement to the UN Sub-Commission on the Prevention of Discrimination and the Protection of Minorities suggested that 'the children are from the lowest socio-economic group of Iranian society, almost all from rural villages. . . . They form groups called *bassaidji* meaning mobilization of the disinherited' (quoted in Woods, 1986).

In October 1982, a decree allowed children of 12 or over, who wished to enlist, to join the army without permission of their parents. The pressure on boys to enlist is graphically described by Paul Derian: 'Sound trucks rolled through the streets urging children to volunteer for srvice. Local mullahs were given quotas of children to recruit. The youngsters were bombarded with appeals to their patriotic and religious beliefs.' (*International Herald Tribune*, 18 July 1984). Women have been known to visit schools to ask the children to avenge the death of their husbands, and children have been officially praised for doing so (Woods, 1986). As a further pressure on conscription, in 1983 the Parliament passed a tough new law against draft dodgers, effectively stripping them of their civil rights, and even threatening to strip them of their food rations. It has been suggested that the regime in Iran found it convenient to use conscription as a safety valve: for those who join the army do not swell the ranks of the unemployed and the discontented. This is, of course, an old strategy but one difficult for outsiders to counter, as Iran is not a signatory of the Geneva Conventions.

As we have seen the Geneva Conventions apply to international conflicts, but children are also increasingly being caught up in internal wars. In one of the oldest conflicts in Africa, there were

reports that the Ethiopian government was press-ganging 14-year-old boys into the army in the war in north-western Eritrea (*Observer*, 5 June 1988). Meanwhile, the role of children in Uganda's National Resistance Army, which came to power in January 1986 after a five-year war, has been the subject of much debate. The guerrilla war which culminated in the victory of Yoweri Museveni's NRA was without precedent in post-colonial Africa. For the first time a guerrilla army had seized power without external help, and child soldiers were a significant part of this force. UNICEF estimated that around 10 per cent of the NRA was comprised of children under 15 years old. Indeed this 'boys' own army' was unusual by any standards. The NRA came to resemble a mobile orphanage since so many of the young guerrillas had joined after being driven from their home by the atrocities committed by government troops after 1983, which left an estimated 200,000 people dead and displaced another 180,000.

Many young boys were orphaned by the massive counter-insurgency campaign in the now notorious Luwero triangle, just north of the capital Kampala. Alone and scared, they wandered in the bush until picked up by the NRA. Subsequently, NRA officers 'adopted' these children and after basic training they would cook and clean, run errands, help watch and go ahead of patrols to gather intelligence. But as the NRA acquired more weapons they began to arm boys as young as eight years. Most boys received captured Kalashnikovs, which because of their size and lightness, seem tailor-made for child soldiers. As the war intensified in late 1985, every available soldier was pressed into action, including the child soldiers. A major offensive was mounted on 17 January 1986, and Kampala fell on 26 January to the NRA in which the child soldiers formed a highly visible element.

The war having been won, attention turned to the future of these child soldiers. UNICEF had opened a dialogue with the NRA leadership on the issue of child soldiers as early as October 1985 and resumed it on 17 January 1986. But no agreement was reached, in spite of discussions that were pursued until July 1986. Cole P. Dodge, the UNICEF Representative in Uganda, who was

A ten-year-old NRA soldier
(*Source*: UNICEF)

Two NRA soldiers, aged seven and ten
(*Source*: UNICEF)

principally involved in the discussions with the government over
the future rehabilitation of the child soldiers, felt that there were
two main options open to the NRA. The first was to keep the
children in the army and provide for their education within the
military itself. The arguments for this option included the fact that
for those children without known parents the NRA had become
their home. They had no wish to leave and they represented the
potential to improve the quality of the NRA as they matured. The
second option was to take the child soldiers out of the army and
enrol them in civilian schools. The schools would provide a

minimum of primary schooling plus one or two skills. By going into civilian schools the children would be given the option of later choosing between a career in the army or civilian life.

The question, therefore, centred on what kind of schooling was appropriate for these children, who are perhaps the key to the country's future if they become its leaders. The government showed an early preference for the first option, while Ugandan church leaders and UNICEF preferred sending the children to civilian schools. Yoweri Museveni and other NRA officers felt that too much fuss was being made by the Western media and the development agencies over the child soldiers. They pointed out that the Geneva Conventions were written largely by Western countries and that they did not apply to Uganda's situation. Museveni, in particular asserted that children in Uganda are taught to fight with sticks and to defend livestock from predators from the age of four, and that it is traditional in Africa for young children to learn how to fight with sticks, spears and arrows. Modern weapons are but an extension of these traditional values. But as Dodge countered: 'There is a big difference between a spear and an automatic weapon. Traditional values will break down very quickly if young children bear arms within this country' (*Sunday Nation*, 16 March 1986). Child soldiers in Uganda have reversed the traditional power relations between generations. Moreover, though it is true that African children grow up sooner than their contemporaries in Western societies, it is still not known what the long-term psychological impact of war experience will be on child soldiers. Dodge claims, 'there have been no studies of child soldiers, and if Uganda decides to keep the children in the NRA, it is unlikely that we will know how these children fare. If the option for civil schools is chosen, there would be the opportunity to follow the children closely and record their experiences during their schooling years' (*C. S. Quarterly*, 10/4). The debate continued for almost a year before up to 2,000 child soldiers received their demobilization orders. For the moment, the government seems to have won the argument as the youngsters were asked in January 1987 to report to two special military academies at Mbarara, 150 miles south west of Kampala and at Bombo, 20 miles north of the capital, to resume their formal schooling.

Child soldiers are increasingly used in both conventional and guerrilla wars in developing countries and yet we have little or no information on how this affects them. The crucial aspect is that children should have choice and that this might more reasonably be exercised at 18 rather than 15. The cause of child soldiers ought to unite all those working in the field of children's rights and child labour, and any Convention on the Rights of the Child should embody these considerations.

5

Child Labour in Developing Countries:
The Urban Sector

'Where are you off to?' I cried to the ragged band of shoe-shine kids, leaving the central park of Guatemala City. 'We are going to our mother the street,' came the reply as they hurried off through the evening crowd.
Peter Taçon, UNICEF

By the year 2000, the world's urban population is likely to increase by half. This will mark an historic shift, as for the first time the world's urban population will exceed that of rural areas. Should present trends continue, there will be 430 cities of over one million inhabitants; and 45 of the 60 cities with over five million inhabitants will be located in developing countries. By the year 2000, four-fifths of the population growth in developing countries is likely to be concentrated in urban areas (see figures 5.1 and 5.2 and table 5.1).

Much of this population growth in urban settlements in developing countries is due to migration. In most of Africa around 70 per cent of urban population growth is associated with migration from rural areas. This reflects a general pattern throughout the developing world of peasant farmers voting with their feet against the rural way of life. Since independence most developing countries have neglected agriculture and the rural areas in favour of urban-biased strategies, patterned on Western industrial models of development. Agriculture is both hard and ill rewarded. Though it sometimes defies understanding why poor rural migrants find shanty-town squalor preferable to life in the village, the town or city holds out that precious element – hope for a better future.

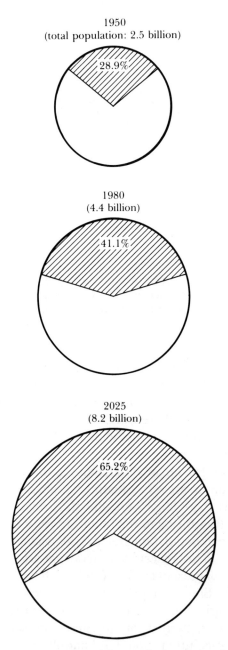

Figure 5.1   Percentage of world population living in urban areas
Source: Agnelli, 1986, p. 20

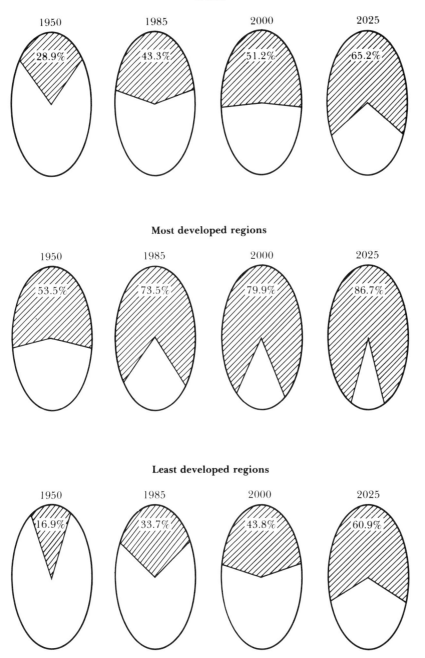

Figure 5.2   Percentage of population living in urban areas
Source: Agnelli, 1986, p. 22

Table 5.1 The world's 25 largest urban agglomerations ranked by population (in millions) in 1970, 1985 and 2000

Rank	Agglomeration/country	Population in 1970	Agglomeration/country	Population in 1985	Agglomeration/country	Population in 2000
1	Greater New York, USA	16.3	Mexico City, Mexico	18.1	Mexico City, Mexico	26.3
2	Tokyo/Yokohama, Japan	14.9	Tokyo/Yokohama, Japan	17.2	São Paulo, Brazil	24.0
3	Shanghai, China	11.4	São Paulo, Brazil	15.9	Tokyo/Yokohama, Japan	17.1
4	London, United Kingdom	10.6	Greater New York, USA	15.3	Calcutta, India	16.6
5	Greater Köln, Federal Republic of Germany	9.3	Shanghai, China	11.8	Greater Bombay, India	16.0
6	Mexico City, Mexico	9.2	Calcutta, India	11.0	Greater New York, USA	15.5
7	Greater Buenos Aires, Argentina	8.5	Greater Buenos Aires, Argentina	10.9	Seoul, Republic of Korea	13.5
8	Greater Los Angeles, USA	8.4	Rio de Janeiro, Brazil	10.4	Shanghai, China	13.5
9	Paris, France	8.3	Seoul, Republic of Korea	10.2	Rio de Janeiro, Brazil	13.3
10	Beijing, China	8.3	Greater Bombay, India	10.1	Delhi, India	13.3

11	São Paulo, Brazil	8.2	Greater Los Angeles USA	10.0	Greater Buenos Aires, Argentina	13.2
12	Osaka/Kobe, Japan	7.6	London, United Kingdom	9.8	Greater Cairo, Egypt	13.2
13	Rio de Janeiro, Brazil	7.2	Beijing, China	9.2	Jakarta, Indonesia	12.8
14	Moscow, USSR	7.1	Greater Köln, Federal Republic of Germany	9.2	Bagdad, Iraq	12.8
15	Calcutta, India	7.1	Paris, France	8.9	Tehran, Iran	12.7
16	Tianjin, China	6.9	Moscow, USSR	8.7	Karachi, Pakistan	12.2
17	Greater Chicago, USA	6.8	Greater Cairo, Egypt	8.5	Istanbul, Turkey	11.9
18	Greater Bombay, India	5.9	Osaka/Kobe, Japan	8.0	Greater Los Angeles	11.2
19	Milan, Italy	5.6	Jakarta, Indonesia	7.9	Dhaka, Bangladesh	11.2
20	Seoul, Republic of Korea	5.4	Tianjin, China	7.8	Manila, Philippines	11.1
21	Greater Cairo, Egypt	5.4	Delhi, India	7.4	Beijing, China	10.8
22	Jakarta, Indonesia	4.5	Bagdad, Iraq	7.2	Moscow, USSR	10.1
23	Greater Philadelphia, USA	4.0	Tehran, Iran	7.2	Bangkok, Thailand	9.5
24	Detroit, USA	4.0	Manila, Philippines	7.0	Tianjin, China	9.2
25	Leningrad, USSR	4.0	Milan, Italy	7.0	Paris, France	9.2

Source: Agnelli, 1986, p. 23

Urbanization has brought with it a qualitative change in the nature of children's work. Child work in an urban context is highly diverse, ranging between intra-family work to apprenticeship outside the family, domestic service, wage labour, odd jobs and errands, and independent activities in the street. In urban areas the spectrum of the child/adult relationship can embrace, at one end, working with parents in such income-generating tasks as making hand-rolled cigarettes, weaving straw and packaging home-made craft products. At the other end of the spectrum, the working child may be almost invisible, as in the case of poor migrant girls sold into virtual slavery as sweatshop workers or as prostitutes. Less dramatic, but even more pervasive, is the plight of child domestic workers, often sent by their parents in the rural areas to distant 'relatives' in the cities, where they remain unpaid or poorly paid in return for their room and board. Between these extremes are the more typical urban child workers living with their families on construction sites, working in factories, shops and restaurants. Then, there are the petty, so called 'marginal' activities, of shoe shining, looking after and washing cars, and other casual means of scraping a meagre living on the street.

For newly arrived rural migrants and the other poor in the marginal settlements which ring most cities in the developing world, child work is an essential part of their survival strategy. Nevertheless, it is urban child labour that gives international development agencies the most grounds for concern: 'It is this radical transformation in the nature and forms of children's work with its concomitant harmful effects on the children concerned that makes child labour an even more pressing problem and a compelling cause for international concern' (Blanchard, 1983, p. 10).

Many of the survival activities of poor urban dwellers and their children are what Rodgers and Standing term 'marginal economic activities'. This category appears merely residual within their overall typology and reflects a tendency by economists to ignore the informal as opposed to the formal economic sector. Such informal economic activities have not been, therefore, subject to rigorous analysis, though they have been given considerable media treatment. Perhaps this is yet another example of what Dudley Seers used to call 'the economics of the special case' – another failure to examine the typical case. And yet as the ILO has revealed, approximately 1,000 million people in the cities of the developing world are directly or indirectly dependent on the informal sector for their livelihood. This number is growing steadily as an estimated five in ten of new entrants to the urban labour-market attempt to set up their own businesses. In Central America the informal sector accounts for 29 per cent of all urban jobs, in Africa 60 per cent. In income terms, the informal sector constitutes between a quarter to one-third of income generated by urban dwellers (ILO, 1986).

The problem of street children is the most visible part of the child labour problem. For that reason, it is often the most officially sensitive aspect of child labour in developing countries and at the same time the most attractive focus for development agencies. Indeed, street children have had an age-old fascination. One only has to think back to Charles Dickens's *Oliver Twist* or to Victor Hugo's *Les Misérables* to realize the universal appeal of the 'street urchin' to the artist, and in our own century to the popular media. In the nineteenth century street children were an accepted feature of the urban landscape, though one which gave rise to social concern. In Britain, as early as the 1840s, Shaftesbury was alarmed by what he termed 'street arabs'. In the United States the extreme proposals of the American Revd Charles Brace were instrumental in the deportation of some 90,000 street children between 1853 and 1890, from the North-East to the Mid-West, where they were placed in foster homes as farm hands. The Reverend Brace writing in 1853 still echoes many contemporary attitudes to street children:

> There are no dangers to the value of property or to the permanency of our institutions so great as those from the existence of a class of vagabond, ignorant, ungoverned children. This 'dangerous class' has not begun to show itself, as it will in eight or ten years, when these boys and girls are matured . . . Then let society beware, when the outcast, vicious, reckless multitude of New York boys swarming now in every foul alley and low street, come to know their power, and use it. (Agnelli, 1986, p. 46)

Street children are, at one and the same time, exotic and potentially subversive for what they represent. At the very least they are an embarrassment, a highly visible evidence of a dual society in which extreme wealth is juxtaposed with extreme poverty. Here it is the typical powder keg of the developing world; governments are overthrown in the cities, not in the rural areas.

The problem of street children has, on the whole, been defined by popular stereotypes with little in the way of a scientific discourse of the issue. In its place are those popular images which enable everyone in Colombia to know what a *gamin* is; or in Peru to know what a *pájarao frutero* (fruit bird) is, or in Zaire what a *moineaux* (sparrow) is. Such public knowledge is fed by the media, in particular via such films as Buñuel's *Los Olivdados* (The Forgotten Ones, 1950) set in Mexico City; the more recent *Pixote* (Hector Babenco, 1981) set in Brazil; and even *Streetwise* (1985) set in Seattle, USA.

Defining such an heterogeneous group is problematic. A popular definition of street children emanates from the Geneva based International Catholic Child Bureau:

> Street children are those for whom the street (in the widest sense of the word i.e. unoccupied dwellings, waste land, etc.) more than their family, has become their real home, a situation in which there is no protection, supervision or direction from responsible adults. (Quoted in UNICEF, Ideas Forum, 1982)

This definition, in fact, describes the extreme condition of abandonment. In its 1986 Executive Board Paper, UNICEF suggested that the term 'street children' should refer to all children who work in the streets of urban areas, without reference to the time they spend there or to the reasons for being there (UNICEF, 1986c, p. 15).

The UNICEF paper also set out a general typology of working and street children, inspired by Peter Taçon. The typology makes a three-fold distinction between:

Group A – Children with continuous contact with their family.
Group B – Children with occasional contact with their family.
Group C – Children without contact with their family.

Despite stereotypes to the contrary, most urban child workers, like their counterparts in the villages, spend most nights with their families or relatives. Unlike most rural children, many urban child workers are either under the supervision of employers outside of the family, or are in business for themselves on the streets. But a growing

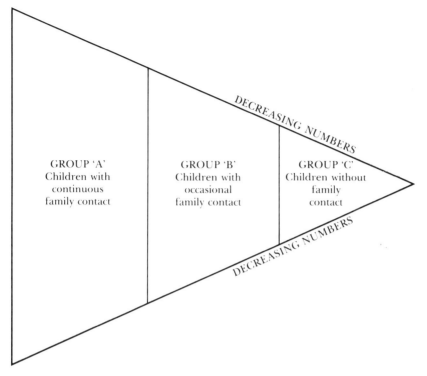

Figure 5.3   Groupings of children
Source: UNICEF, 1986c, p. 13

percentage of these working children spend all of their days and some of their nights sleeping on the streets or in public places. These are *children on the street*. They are not abandoned, but extreme poverty has forced them out of their homes to become, at least partially, self-supporting. These children are easy to spot in any central city, particularly in Latin America, as they go about shining shoes, washing cars and selling cigarettes. Many will be attending school on a shift basis, and their street trading will be helping to pay their fees, as well as contributing to family income.

Most poor communities have a smaller group of children who have severed contact with family and relatives. These are what UNICEF calls *children of the street*. In extreme circumstances, as was recently reported in Maputo, Mozambique, a third of street children may be these abandoned children. Based on its Latin American experience, UNICEF suggests that the proportional breakdown between these groups is as follows:

Group A: 75 per cent candidates for the streets.
Group B: 20 per cent children on the streets.
Group C: 5 per cent children of the streets.

It is dangerous both to aggregate street children and to suggest that they are a totally disorganized group. Street life is not unstructured. Many street activities are controlled by 'territory', best exemplified by the street gang. Perhaps the best known example of the street gang is the *gallada* of Bogotá. This is a well structured and efficient platoon of five or ten boys led by the oldest and strongest member, who is often armed. It is the leader who defends the young, finds lucrative places for members to work and knows safe places to sleep. The *gallada* has its own roles, such as snatching bags, stealing bicycles, guarding territory or faking tears when begging.

Galladas in Bogotá go back to at least 1860 and Colombia might indeed be called the world capital of street children. The country's leading daily newpaper *El Tiempo*, carries a daily comic strip on *gamines*, and they have inspired soap operas on radio and TV and even a ballet by the National Company! Their emotional appeal makes them, in addition, good fodder for politicians. They remain, perhaps, the best documented tribe of the urban jungle.

If street life has its own hierarchies and organizational structures it also has a fluidity which can make appeareances deceptive. Not all 'streetwise' children are necessarily street children. Many children move between categories of work in the urban sector. A typical example is of a 12-year-old boy shoe shining outside the Lima Sheraton from 2 p.m. to 6 p.m. every day in 1982. He began his shoe shining career at the age of eight, and was using his earnings to put himself through primary school. He attended in the morning shift at school and in about a year's time he expected to hand on his *cajón* (box) to his younger brother. This was a family tradition and this boy would, after 12, try to concentrate on his studies and work in a workshop during school holidays. Another example is the case of Carlos, a 16-year-old, who in 1982 was on probation in Lima for stealing watches. He had begun his working life around the age of seven helping his bricklayer father at his work. Then, when he was 12, he stopped attending school and began to help a woman who sold fish in the market place. When he was 13 had had a brief spell earning a wage in a bookshop, before spending a year helping his mother sell alfalfa. In between, there were short spells where he shined shoes. When he was big enough to defend himself he joined an older brother who was already part of a gang which guarded and cleaned cars. This is where he learned that picking pockets and stealing watches was more lucrative than working washing cars (ASS, 1984b, p. 42). This career reveals the extent to which the residual 'marginal' category needs further refining (perhaps into informal, casual and outcast) and also shows the importance of age for children's work. For some occupations a critical stage of development must be reached. Children who sell, whether on the streets or in a market, need to be able to do simple addition. Children who work in car cleaning gangs must be strong enough to defend their territory. The urban jungle is not as disorganized as it may first appear.

Given the approximate nature of the definition of 'street children' no objective global statistics exist. Frequently, too, because of their lower profile and visibility, as well as official embarrassment, girls are ignored in the assessment of numbers. A range of estimates have been put forward for global figures: 80 million (UNICEF, 1986c); 60

Street child, Lima, Peru
(*Source*: UNICEF)

Girl newspaper seller, Colombia
(*Source*: UNICEF)

million (WHO in ASS, 1984b). Half of this figure is usually taken to
be the estimate for Latin America. This emphasis on Latin America
may be simply a reflection of the more easily accessible data. Within
Latin America the countries most affected appear to be Brazil,
Colombia and Mexico, though there is a growing incidence in Peru
and Chile, as a result of economic pressures, and the effect of
internal conflicts forcing people out of the rural areas. In Africa the
numbers of street children are increasing with the combined effects
of famine and war. In Khartoum, where the phenomenon was
virtually unknown, there are an estimated 20,000 street children.
Information on Asia is scarce and is confused by the existence of
pavement communities, as in India. Nevertheless, given rapid

Girl shoe-shining, Ecuador
(*Source*: UNICEF)

Street children, Brazil
(*Source*: UNICEF)

urbanization the problem may well be comparable to Latin America. The ASS (1985) has made one of the few attempts at a more systematic projection, both for Latin America and for the incidence of street children world-wide (see table 5.2).

Table 5.2 shows that if there were indeed 50 million street children in Latin America, this would mean that nearly a third of the total of 158 million children in the region would have their permanent home in the streets. This can hardly be the case, for all existing country-wide studies of child labour place the economically active child population at around one-quarter to one-third of the total, including the vast majority who work within households and in agriculture. An estimate which would include all street activities including casual work and those who work for family members, reveals that probably about one-third of economically active children are engaged in these occupations. Various studies of Latin American cities indicate that around one-quarter of the children working in the streets live outside of a family structure, giving a total of just over four million for Latin America and the Caribbean.

Using the 1984 UNICEF Report *The State of the World's Children*, the ASS has made a further estimate of the world incidence of street children. This self-confessed *ad hoc* estimate starts from the premise

Table 5.2 Estimates of working children in Latin America and the Caribbean, 1983 – in '000s

	Total population[a]	Child population[b]	Economically active children[c]	Street children[d]	'Abandoned' children[e]
Caribbean (including Guyana and Surinam)	21,536	10,983	3,661	1,098	275
Latin America	312,263	158,744	52,914	15,829	3,969
Total	333,799	169,727	56,575	16,927	4,244

[a] Taken from *Whitaker's Almanack*, 1983. Most figures refer to 1980s censuses, but a few are earlier and some are estimates.

[b] Under 15 years of age; calculated as 51% of total population.

[c] Most studies place this as one-quarter to one-third of the child population. The figure given here includes children working within the family home and in seasonal agricultural labour.

[d] Probably an overestimate to include all children who work in the street, some with family members and many only casually.

[e] Based on figures from various latin American cities, which indicate that around one-quarter of the children working in the streets live outside family structures.

Source: Anti-Slavery Society, 1985, p. 44

that there will be some relationship between the infant mortality rate and child welfare in general, and, therefore, the population figures for countries with high, low and medium rates of infant mortality are aggregated, as in UNICEF 1984. The populations of socialist countries are not included because they do not recognize the existence of the problem. The urban population is derived from the mean percentage of the population urbanized in each group. As street children are usually found in the 5–15 years age group, a total urban child population in this age group is calculated using rather crude percentages. The number of economically active children in each group is taken to be about one-third, as this tends to conform with most child labour studies. As not all urban children engage in street work, it is estimated that only one-third will be *children on the street*. The final estimate that one-third of these will be *children of the street* is taken from the pyramid model from Peter Taçon. The final figure of 7.7 million abandoned street children does not include the runaway population of the developed world, which involves a different problem of estimation. The ASS concludes that caution should be used in comparing the results of tables 5.2 and 5.3 because they are derived from different bases. They do show that Latin America does, in fact, contain 50 per cent of the world's street children. Although the figures are not definitive, they are a basis for more rigorous statistical work. (See table 5.3.)

According to the Independent Commission on International Humanitarian Issues (ICIHI) '. . . part of the tragedy of street children may indeed be that they are far less attractive, as objects of compassion, than many others.' (Agnelli, 1986, p. 71). This seems at variance with the well-recorded exoticism factor already noted, which has led development agencies into open competition to provide projects for them, as in Bogotá (Isabel King, private communication). I have also been struck by the romantic fascination they seem to hold for some development workers, as one observes the photo montages of street children on home and office walls and even models of the 'little heroes' of the urban poor on office desks!

In 1982 an inter-NGO programme was set up in Geneva, but after three years was not considered much of a success, and in 1985 a new international NGO was announced, based in Guatemala City, called 'ChildHope'. Between 1982 and 1985 the inter-NGO programme identified 150 street children projects world-wide – a wild underestimate, as Brazil alone is thought to have 300 projects.

Table 5.3 An estimate of the number of street children world-wide

Infant mortality rate (per '000)	Total population (millions) (1981)	% of population urbanized (1981)	Urban population (millions)	Urban child population aged 5–15 years (millions)	Economically active urban children (millions)	Children on the street (millions)	Children of the street (millions)
Over 100	1,301.9	21	273.4	90.2 (33%)	29.8	9.8	3.2
60–100	657.1	41	269.4	89.9 (33%)	29.3	9.7	3.2
26–50 (excluding socialist)	322.3	51	164.4	36.2 (22%)	11.9	3.9	1.3
Under 25 (excluding socialist)	741.0	76	563.2	61.9 (11%)	–	–	–
Socialist	1,438.7	–	–	–	–	–	–
Total	–	–	–	–	71.0	23.4	7.7

Source: Anti-Slavery Society, 1985, p. 44

In policy approaches to the problem in Latin America there is often a tension between government policies, which lay stress on institutional care, and those of NGOs and the international development agencies, which place the emphasis on preventing action through community care. The present trend in project design for street children is towards the non-residential, community-based project which uses work itself, under protected conditions, as the agent of socialization. This type of project is intended for children in Group B – children not completely estranged from their families, but in danger of becoming so. It is much cheaper than residential care, and can cater for far greater numbers of children. Some projects based upon the production of handicrafts, textiles, ceramics, or furniture are almost self-sufficient. This model has been pioneered by NGOs and, in recent years, has been actively advocated by UNICEF as an alternative to state-run institutions.

The Republica Do Pequeño Vendedor (Republic of Young Tradesmen) in Belém, Brazil, is typical of this community-based approach. Its clients are about 500 car-washers, coffee-sellers, or newspaper and shoe-shine boys. They congregate at noon in two restaurants, which provide a subsidized lunch – a typical contact and entry point in such projects. The children are recruited by teams of volunteers who go out once a week to find them and to make contact with their families to see what their real needs are. The project recycles discarded goods such as old refrigerators, armchairs, bicycles and other jumble donated once a year. Items in saleable condition are immediately disposed of to provide general funds for the project. Those requiring repair or refurbishment are distributed to the project workshops where they are reconditioned by the team of young apprentices and sold at affordable prices to poor families.

Those *children of the street* who are more alienated require a different approach. The Foundation of Youth Counselling in Bogotá, commonly known as 'Bosconia/La Florida', is an innovative attempt to meet the needs of these children. Completed in 1981, it is spread over a number of sites. In order to penetrate the gangs it has evolved a sequence of situations of non-, partly and fully residential, corresponding roughly to different stages of psychological development. Contact is made on the streets where children are invited into a courtyard for lunch, to wash and to play games. Later for those who show interest, a simple dormitory provides shelter for the night.

From this semi-residential regime, the child moves to a more elaborate, full-time programme including group therapy, basic literacy, training and non-directive learning. Work is central to the educational programme, and is viewed as a positive instrument for learning and socialization. After a month-long Leadership Training Course, the children become citizens of the La Florida Boys Town, a complex of buildings in an attractive rural setting where they are introduced to a system of self-government. 'La Republica de los Muchachos' has its own written constitution, with an elected Mayor and Governing Council. The final stage takes the form of an industrial firm, Industrias Bosconia, producing a variety of metal components, including solar heating panels. Work becomes humanized and economically practical.

These examples stress how vital initial contacts are in building confidence. Street educators have played a very important role in some of these local initiatives. Although this approach goes back at least to the last century with the work of Don Bosco in Italy, it has recently grown in Latin America. The street educator is often a former street child who ultimately aims to involve children in programmes of non-formal education, counselling and job support.

Counselling, São José dos Campos, Brazil
(*Source*: UNICEF)

As UNICEF pointed out in its 1986 Paper, this approach to reaching street children at their work site should be explored fully, but with one vital caveat, 'it is a means, not an end in itself. It is important to avoid the fallacy of institutionalizing the street itself.' (1986c, p. 27).

But one of the problems of these community-based models is that they are less serviceable, if at all, with totally abandoned children. This is why the 'Republic of Young Tradesmen' is being watched with much interest to see whether it is transferable to other non-Latin American contexts. One vehicle for such technical transfers are the intergovernmental agencies. Here UNICEF stands out, particularly for its work since 1982. The ICHI report suggests that UNICEF's advocacy work in Brazil, 'provides a text-book example of how a UN agency can change mentalities, provoke initiatives and withdraw once the ball is rolling' (Agnelli, 1986, p. 82).

This partnership began in May 1982 when the Brazilian Ministry of Social Assistance and Welfare requested that UNICEF share in the development of a two-year project on 'Alternative Services for Street Children'. During this pilot phase meetings attended by government officials, NGOs, religious leaders, educators and employers were convened in some 300 urban and peri-urban communities. In almost every case this led to a project run by NGOs under the auspices of the National Child Welfare Agency (FUNABEM). As a result of this partnership. Brazil is so far the only country in the world to have a coherent national policy on street children, with a level of public awareness and debate unmatched elsewhere (Agnelli, 1986, p. 82). But it should be made clear that UNICEF's role has largely been one of a catalyst for these community-based projects. UNICEF has not been able to devote as much of its resources to the problem as it both deserves and as the agency would like. Between 1983 and 1986 UNICEF allocated only $500,000 from its general resources for a regional progamme to assist street children, though it helped to raise a further $2 million through its national committee system for special 'noted' projects. The 1986 Executive Board affirmed this general strategy and endorsed UNICEF's status as a leading agency for street children world-wide. Its experience in Brazil has been gradually transferred to Colombia, Mexico, Kenya, Mozambique, the Philippines and Thailand. And yet a critical need to evaluate the impact of such projects, in both quantitative and qualitative terms, remains largely unfulfilled. Any UN agency faces the constraint of national government willingness to co-operate. In Brazil, UNICEF found a sympathetic ear, but in Peru the wife of the new President launched a campaign in the summer of 1985 to fund children's homes. A year later the streets of Lima were ominously empty of street children. Street children can, when the need arises, be swept off the street in cosmetic operations.

Other UN agencies could and should follow UNICEF's lead. The ILO appears now to be taking a stronger interest in the informal sector. UNESCO could play a catalytic role in promoting street-based educational initiatives. In fact there is an urgent need in this field, as with the whole problem of child labour, for the international agencies to co-ordinate their approaches. So far it has been the NGOs who have shown the most initiative in pioneering strategies to meet the needs of street children. In any strategy the first need is to recognize the problem, and not all countries are as candid and open to external support as Brazil and Colombia. There are three possible strategies for working with street children – containment, cure and prevention. As Ennew points out only the first two are usually attempted (1986b). Containment takes the form of conventional institutional care, often repressive, as shown in the Brazilian film *Pixote*. Such institutions are usually overcrowded and staffed by inadequately trained and overworked staff. The cure approach involves, as we have seen in the case studies, the weaning away of children from street life, gradually re-introducing them to education and regular work patterns. This seems to be more cost-effective, especially when combined with an out-reach, street educator programme. Prevention – stopping the children appearing on the streets in the first place – is the least explored strategy. This is largely due to the perception that poverty is the root cause of family disintegration and is beyond eradication. But this cannot be a sufficient argument. As Ennew suggests, Cuba used to have an enormous street child population which has now disappeared, despite the fact that the country is not much wealthier now than it was before the revolution. Some of the poorest families stay together and would not dream of letting their children loose on the streets. Such family dynamics, as prosaic as love and duty, clearly count and must be taken seriously before we can have adequate explanations of the complex reasons behind a child's decision to leave home and live on the streets (Ennew, 1986b). Finally, we have assumed all along that children are the passive recipients of the good works of adults. However, the whole field of children's rights is beginning to look at the potential for self-advocacy, in which groups of children with a shared perspective or problem unite to promote their cause (Boyden, 1985, p. 5).

Interesting examples of such self-advocacy strategies have emerged, again from Latin America. The first example not surprisingly emanates from Brazil. During 26–8 May 1986, the first national conference for street children was held in Brasilia. It brought together 432 street children from different regions of the country. The delegates, ranging from 8 to 16 years of age, were selected by their colleagues by ballot. The conference and the selection of the delegates was organized by the National Movement of Street Children, an NGO that grew out of a community-based project supported by UNICEF and FUNABEM. Only a few adults were invited to the conference which discussed the themes of work, education, violence, family, political organization and health. The violence workshop was by far the most popular and dealt in particular with police violence. Most delegates had experienced violence and questions included:

'Why do we girls have to have sex with the police to get out of
    prison?'
'Why do the police have the right to beat minors?'

These themes had been chosen by the children themselves through a series of pre-meetings organized throughout the country. At a closing ceremony the children presented short plays that summarized the conference's conclusions. The conference was well covered by the media with over 15 pages in newspapers and magazines, an hour on TV and innumerable radio items and wire service stories that found their way to Europe. 'Now Brazil will know what we are like,' said one 15-year-old girl. The conclusions of the meetings were sent out to senators and the media. The delegates returned to their cities and towns to discuss their conclusions and demands covering: a law against violent treatment, better schools, free school books, better pay for parents, laws governing children's work and pay, and even a trade union for child workers. Whether or not such a conference actually has the desired political impact is too early to say, but its more enduring value is that it demonstrates that children can be both the end and the means of advocacy.

In Peru there exists an older national organization of working children called MANTHOC, established under Catholic lay auspices in 1977. It, too, has held national conferences and has put forward as one of its aims the loosening of the institutional rigidities of urban schools to enable street children to combine schooling with their need to work. These children, in what UNICEF calls 'especially difficult circumstances', are beginning to command growing national and international attention, as witnessed by the International Year of Shelter for the Homeless (1987), the ICHI Report, and the Executive Board Paper of UNICEF, both in 1986. At least their visibility commands attention, not so the many other urban work activities to which we must now turn.

If street children are the most visible urban child work activity, then: '. . . the most hidden activity about which the least is known in statistical terms is domestic labour which is more frequently carried out by girls.' (ASS, 1984a, p. 1). Domestic labour, like the informal sector, receives little attention because it is thought not to be productive. And yet, it has been estimated that household services by housewives and domestic servants can be valued at 40 per cent or more of the GNP in developing countries (ASS, 1984a, p. 1). It is neglected, too, because domestic labour is concealed in the home. Nevertheless, it is, according to Boudhiba, the most widespread and least researched abuse of child work. These are the 'maids-of-all work' in situations of virtual slavery. The abuse is often disguised through the misuse of apparently respectable fictitious family relationships, such as adopting and fostering. Domestic workers are, moreover, usually poor girls from the rural areas who are new to the urban environment and therefore particularly isolated and unable to organize with others.

The role and existence of domestic workers appears to be of universal symbolic importance to middle-class families in developing countries. In the newly independent countries of Africa it is the new middle classes who see in domestic servants a way of emulating colonial lifestyles. Although this form of child work abuse can be found in most of the developing world, it is Latin America which provides clear examples of the cultural context in which child domestic workers are exploited. Three factors combine to produce the typical situation of exploitation:

1 A polarized class structure, in which a relatively numerous wealthy middle class has a virtual monopoly, this distinction is

further compounded by a parallel division between urban and rural populations, and between those of European descent and an indigenous Indian population.

2   The ethos of 'machismo' which oppresses women, relegating them to household activities and giving men both economic and political power. The patriarchal family is so dominant that any form of family relationship, real or fictive, appears to be legally binding and female minors are particularly powerless.

3   The prevalence of the system of patron–client relationships, epitomized in god-parenthood, in which fictitious family relationships are used to gain advantages of various kinds.

The ASS in its report to the United Nations Working Group on Slavery in 1984 cited the examples of child domestics in Brazil, the Dominican Republic and Peru. The Report suggested that in Brazil there were some areas in which nearly one-third of the domestic workers were children. These workers were marginals without legal protection. As early as the age of three or four, children may be farmed out to other households, their relationship to its members almost always modelled on fictitious kinship and represented in hospitality, adoption or god-parenthood. In some cases there is a kin link, but this is usually distant and the child will not be treated as a family member, despite perhaps being addressed by a kin term, such as 'cousin'. The children are usually unpaid because they have to learn domestic tasks. But in some cases they work to pay off the debt of a biological parent. The enduring tie is not between the child and its 'adoptive' parent or 'god-parent', but between the two families, a relationship which entails assumed obligations over debts on both sides. Such children can be termed 'super-exploited': unpaid, overworked and unprotected by either real or fictive parents.

In the Dominican Republic the predominant type of domestic servant is the type known as *puerta cerrada* (closed door). Over two-thirds of the female domestics in Santa Domingo are migrants from the rural areas, which exacerbates their isolation. The isolation of young girl domestics from both the family with which they live and the wider society is, according to the ASS, almost total. These girls may only have a small dark 'service room' in which to sleep. But more often than not they have to sleep where they can in the yard or kitchen, without the company of other domestics, because usually

Girls doing domestic work, Karachi, Pakistan
(*Source*: UNICEF)

only one maid-of-all work is kept. They eat different food to the family, at different hours and work up to 72 hours a week. These girls therefore have little opportunity to meet and combine with others in the same situation.

In Lima, Peru, nearly 90 per cent of all domestic workers are migrants from the rural areas, and according to the ASS, about 12 per cent are aged between seven and 14 and over a third are in the 15 to 19 age group. A great many arrive in the city as young children under 'adoption' or 'god-parenthood' arrangements. Their rural parents entrust them to a third party in the hope that they will find work and education in the city. Once arrived, they receive little pay and are often ill-treated or overworked; moreover, their situation as fictitious family members has ironic consequences. The employing family may rationalize virtual imprisonment in the home as caring for the girl's morals, but traditionally they are available to the sons of the family. If they become pregnant, however, they will be turned out, forcing many of them into prostitution to care for their illegitimate children. Should they run away, the employing 'parents' as 'guardians' are able to take legal steps to have them returned to 'family' care and control.

Domestic workers have few rights secured by law, which guarantees eight hours rest at night. Wages are arbitrary, about a third of those earned by street vendors, unskilled labourers or workers in other service industries. The need for the middle class to acquire maids has led to an increasing tendency to seek 'adoptive daughters', 'distant cousins', or 'god-daughters', from rural areas. As family members these girls are unprotected by the Children's Legal Code or by labour law. Moreover, the racist bias in Peruvian society prevents these rural Indian girls from being aware of, or fighting for, their rights.

This racial bias in domestic work is perhaps best exemplified in South Africa. In both the rural and urban areas of South Africa, black girls are frequently involved in domestic duties. In research into domestic workers in Eastern Cape Province by Jacklyn Cork (1980), 90 per cent said that they had started their first job as 'young girls' of 18 years and under. Some had started working when they were 11 or 12 as 'nannies', looking after small white children. To one question, 'At what age did you start your first job?', a woman replied: 'Don't know, I've been a slave for a long time' (quoted in ASS, 1983, p. 59). The ASS report of 1983 stated that, 'Domestic service in South Africa is both a source of child employment and of child neglect.' (p. 60). Adult domestic workers, because of their work demands, are forced to neglect their own children while looking after those of their employers. The exploitation of coloured child domestics was documented by the press for Western Cape in 1976–7. There it was suggested that it was a common practice for businessmen to visit rural areas to recruit children who were often no more than ten or 11 years old. In a follow-up in 1980 by the ASS it was claimed that this recruitment practice still continued. Domestic workers have no legislation to protect them so there is usually no discussion of wages or of working conditions. So accounts of 'slave wages' and 'child slavery' abound in the media with suggestions that children are traded in urban areas.

As we have already seen child prostitution is an aspect of street life. It is also a feature of growing tourist development upon which many developing countries are heavily dependent. This form of super-exploitation of children is poorly researched for the obvious reasons that it is both illegal and unsavoury. Turning children into a commodity is nowhere better exampled than in prostitution, which, as its Latin root *prostituere* suggests, is to offer for public sale and profit an individual's sexuality. Ennew suggests prostitution can be viewed as part of a wider system of exploitation '. . . in which rich exploit poor, males, females, whites, other ethnic groups and adults, children' (Ennew, 1986a, p. 70). As with other commodities, prostitution is subject to a price mechanism in which youth may raise the price. In any analysis of the economics of child sexuality a distinction must be made between pre-pubertal child prostitutes and post-pubertal minors who are involved in prostitution (Ennew, 1986a, p. 81). Most of the available evidence about child prostitutes refers to young people who have not reached the age of majority and not to pre-pubertal children. The market for young children may, according to Ennew, be overstated and is not necessarily the basis for a profitable industry (1986a, p. 83). Pre-pubertal child prostitution is found at both ends of the price market. Paedophiliac customers are specifically interested in child sex, but the market is limited. The other market for pre-pubertal sex is associated with the streets. It is those 7.7 million abandoned children who are particularly vulnerable to adult exploitation in the form of cheap sex. Here the customers may not be paedophiliac, but simply men for whom children provide the cheapest partners over whom they can exercise that power which is denied them. Street children may be exploited by adults or youths who act as procurers and provide the children with food, drugs, and a fiction of adult protection. Equally, children may sell their own sexuality directly to casual customers for such mundane items as sweets and cigarettes.

In developing countries the demand for prostitutes has been enhanced by the advent of mass tourism and in some cases of sex tourism. Mass tourism is the modern successor to the more aristocratic Grand Tour which for Boswell and Goethe offered the classic mixture of the exotic and the erotic. The expansion of tourism, rather than elite travel, is the product of workers' holidays and other improvements in the pay and conditions of Western workers, coupled with the technological developments of air travel. With mass tourism has come tourist resorts and the high-pressured selling which distorts national images, so that some of the richest people in rich countries can visit some of the poorest people in poor countries. The commercialization of sex has also been part of this process, as this widely quoted remark by the then Deputy Prime Minister of Thailand in November 1980 reveals: 'I ask all governors to consider the natural scenery in your provinces, together with some forms of entertainment that some of you might consider disgusting and shameful because they are forms of sexual entertainment that attract tourists. . . . We must do this because we have to consider the jobs that will be created for the people' (quoted in Ennew, 1986a, p. 99). This dependence upon tourism encourages exploitation. Tourism accounts for the third largest item in Thailand's GNP and for the Philippines it is the fourth largest item. Tour operators are not slow either to exploit the erotic as well as the exotic. In the late 1970s and 1980s the Spartacus Gay Guides published in Amsterdam provided male homosexual tourists with up-to-date advice about the availability of boys. Boys are also an attraction to mature women. The largest group of Africans in Sweden consist of some 1500 Gambian boys imported by mature Swedish women who befriend them on holiday (*Observer*, 30 October 1988).

Many agencies arrange package holidays in which sexual experiences are an explicit part of the arrangement, indeed they may be the only reason for the journey. This is particularly the case for tourists travelling from Europe, the United States, Australasia and Japan to south-east Asia. Sex tourism in the region is so ubiquitous that all tourists, regardless of gender, are assumed to require sexual services.

The Japanese still provide most of the demand in the area, supplemented by the American military presence. Until 1980 it was common for groups of up to 200 Japanese males to visit the Philippines on three days' sexual package tours. Thereafter, local protests stemmed the demand, and instead a reverse flow of Filipino women to Japan has occurred. In the case of American demand it was the Korean War, followed by the Vietnam War, which turned many centres in Vietnam, Thailand, the Philippines, Korea and Taiwan into rest and recreation areas. When the war ended, prostitution in Vietnamese bases ceased, but the 7th Fleet's home port, Subic Naval Base, and the rest and recreation centre in Olangapo, both in the Philippines, remain as the largest centres for prostitution in Asia. A total of 7,000 hospitality girls and prostitutes are licensed by the city in return for weekly medical checks (Ennew, 1986a, p. 110).

Organization is not simply the preserve of external agencies. In the Philippines, recruiters from Manila tour the provinces and convince mothers to allow their children to work in a store or restaurant. But upon reaching Manila the rectruiters initiate the child into prostitution (The Filipino Child Link, June 1985). Child prostitution rings often organize sex dens that house child prostitutes to which tourist clients are invited. These rings are also known to have links with foreign groups. This is evidenced by the exposure in 1983 of the Australian Paedophile Support Group's procuring children to Australia on the pretext of foster parents' institutions adopting them.

The substantial assistance to the families of quick cash earnings from child prostitutes act as the triggering factor for parental neglect. Indeed parents may encourage their own children to work as prostitutes. This process may start out as the child being taken along to their income-earning activities, such as vending or begging. In the process, the children are introduced by the mother to pimps. Both the mother and the pimp will thereafter receive shares from the child's earings. In Thailand they have a word for the child recruiter, 'fisherwoman' or child-catcher, who works with the employment agencies clustered around Bangkok's main railway station. They are busiest during January, February and March, which is the dry season in Thailand. It is the time when train loads of children aged eight or even younger arrive in the middle of the night from such impoverished provinces as the north-east. Sometimes the children are alone, sometimes accompanied by other fisherwomen who seek their commodity at source.

Government policies vary from state to state. Generally it is the procuring and traffic aspect which is proscribed rather than prostitution itself. This is reflected in the statutes of the chief international instrument, the 1949 Convention for the Suppression of the Traffic in Persons and of the Prostitution of Others. This came into force in 1951 and by 1982 it had been ratified in 53 states. Some governments simply refuse to accept that the problem exists at all. Remarkably, the Philippines government has in the past taken this stance, claiming that 'it does not exist' because prostitution is prohibited!

The most commonly held image of child labour is that of direct wage labour. This conjures up the classic picture of the Lancashire cotton mills of the early nineteenth century. Wage labour case studies have been, and remain, the easiest and therefore the best documented cases of child labour exploitation. It is for this reason, too, that they form the basis of direct campaigning strategies for the passing of minimum age legislation. But despite the virtual universality of minimum age legislation, child wage labourers continue to exist, particularly in small-scale enterprise – the 'sweat-shops' – which defy the inadequate numbers of factory inspectorates. Abuses of the law in this sector may not simply be a matter of the employment of underage children, but the exploitation of minors through low wages and poor conditions, which would not be tolerated by adult workers.

Few economists have made an independent study of the reasons why it is profitable to use child wage labour. Clearly, children make for an easily disciplined labour force because of their subordinate position in society. For classical economics, because children are immature, smaller and less productive than adults, they are naturally paid less in the marketplace. Other economic theories view women and children as supplementary to the adult male labour force. They participate in the labour-market in order to supplement the inadequate wages of a breadwinner. This makes it possible to pay low wages all round. Children are, therefore, not free in the same sense that an adult is free to sell his or her labour. The economic system forces children to work as does the power relationship exerted by parents.

Gender and seniority, according to Elson (1982), exert indepen-dent force in the labour-market. Even if children become skilled, they cannot be regarded nor paid as 'skilled workers' until they are adult males, in other words 'breadwinners'. Children are, there-fore, enmeshed in three forms of subordination that are interwoven: economic subordination; the social and cultural construction of gender relations; and the power relations of seniority enshrined in law and customs. One should not assume therefore that some jobs are suitable for children. On the contrary, the combination of social and economic logic entails that both jobs and wage systems emerged to suit already existing structures of gender and seniority.

South-east Asia provides some of the best documented examples of child labour in sweatshops, often producing luxury goods for sale in the West. Thailand has an estimated 5,000 unregulated factories (ASS, 1985). And though Thai law prohibits children under 12 from being employed there have been numerous exposures over the years of the sweatshop exploitation of children. In February 1984, a British television documentary, *Rags to Riches*, created a storm with its assertion that there was a direct link between prominent High Street clothing retailers in Britain and the sweated child labour of their Bangkok suppliers and that

> Factory owners shy away from employing girls who have lived in Bangkok for fear that they are too streetwise and can fend for themselves. Poor, illiterate, uneducated farm girls from Thailand's impoverished North and North-East are the employers' choice. They work hard, ask few questions, and don't complain. In effect, buying in Bangkok enables British firms to circumvent over 150 years of British social legislation. (Harriman, 1984)

In another typical case reported in *The Nation* and *Daily Mirror*, 29 April 1986, police rescued 18 girls from a Bangkok textile mill:

> Police rescued 18 girls, most aged 12–14, from a family textile mill in Thonburi area where they were allegedly made to work more than 15 hours a day for almost no pay. The owner of the factory, Mr. Yisiam Sae Lee, 27, was arrested on charges of child slavery and false imprisonment. The police reported that all the girls were from Northeastern provinces and had been sold to the factory on contract by a job placement agency about a year ago. They told the police that they had to work from 5 a.m. to 9 p.m. daily with almost no days off. (*Child Workers in Asia*, vol. 2, no. 2, 1986)

As we have seen in the case of the recruitment of child prostitutes the supply of child workers stems largely from rural to urban migration through different channels, as shown in figure 5.4.

Thailand has both minimum-age and minimum-wage legislation, but both are contravened with impunity. This is hardly surprising. In 1980, there were only 50 inspectors to supervise 15,000 registered industrial establishments in Bangkok. And in addition, there are the illegal units which can only be inspected when the Labour Department receives allegations about them (Banerjee, 1980, p. 29). But, given the small-scale nature of these unregistered units, it is easy for them to shift their operations to avoid detection. Child workers can be passed off as relatives. Labour inspectors can be, and are, bribed

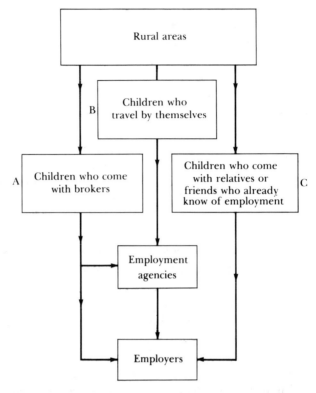

Figure 5.4   The supply of child workers from rural areas
Source: *Child Workers in Asia*, 1986, vol. 2, no. 2, p. 1

by employers. Trade unionism is weak and constrained by the authorities. Nevertheless, Thai NGOs have been active in bringing abuses to light. One focus of their activities has been the campaign for children to be paid the official minimum wage which might encourage employers to substitute adult workers for children. In February 1984, the Central Labour Court ruled, in a case against an employer using illegal child labour, that he had to pay the minimum wage which had previously only been thought to apply to adults.

There is also the 'nimble fingers' theory that children are uniquely suited to certain forms of work and are, therefore, preferred on that account by employers in those industries requiring intricate operations. This is no better exemplified than in the carpet industry, the subject of the Anti-Slavery Society's first major exposé in 1978.

The ASS took Morocco as its case study because the carpet industry was thought to be a large-scale employer of children. The industry was investigated in 1975 with a follow-up visit in 1977. The report of 1978 stated that only in eight of the 62 factories visited were little girls not seen at work (ASS, 1978, p. 9). In 28 factories/workshops at least one-third of the workers were under 12, sometimes as many as three-fifths. These children were often only eight, nine or ten years old. Conditions were bad. Hours were long. Half of the sample exceeded the 48-hour legal maximum for a week's work for adults. Five worked 60–64 hours a week and two 72 hours a week. Wages were meagre with so-called apprentices earning nothing. Some girls had worked for 16 months as unpaid apprentices. This is an example of the corruption of the old craftsman–apprentice structure under which a qualified craftswoman, a *maalema*, supplies her own team and is paid for the work she produces. In turn, she pays her workers as she sees fit.

Originally, the *maalema* worked in her own home with as many as she could manage but rarely exceeding three or four, with up to 20 workers. Many of her workers would be apprentices waiting their turn to become *maalema* and set up on their own. Sometimes these unpaid apprentices were lodged, fed and clothed by the *maalema*. who might take a personal interest in their well-being. On other occasions the apprentices were little more than slaves – it all depended on the character of the *maalema*. The transfer of this sub-contracting system to the factory is detrimental to the children but convenient for the factory owners. The employer pays the *maalema* per square metre worked and has no further responsibility towards the children. He does not know who they are, how old they are, whether they stay one week or several years. Under this system, the sub-contractor has every interest in squeezing the maximum amount of work out of her workers for the minimum possible wages. The *maalema* has absolute control over these child workers and can recruit and discharge them as she likes. The ASS found that the *maalema* system survived in a few state factories as well as most of those in the private sector, where it is the principal cause of child labour abuse. Furthermore, the employment of children was expanding rapidly with the growth of the industry (ASS, p. 57). As is so often the case, child labour is cheap labour, and an important means of keeping costs down for the lucrative export market. At the time of the ASS report, West Germany was the largest importer of

Moroccan rugs as well as a re-exporter throughout Europe. Another unpleasant feature of the industry is the contrast between the well-appointed head office of a rug factory and the dark, cramped, back-street premises of its scattered workshops.

Evidence from India also lends weight to the argument that the demand for child workers in the urban sector has more to do with recruiting the cheapest and most malleable labour available than the need for so-called 'nimble fingers'. A study undertaken by the Madras Institute of Development Studies questioned the contention that the nature of the operations in the notorious match industry called for the use of children (*Indian Workers*, June 1986). An examination of the 17 processes in match manufacturing revealed that children were employed in all 12 of the piece-rated or contracted operations. These were all simple tasks requiring a speed of movement and co-ordination of actions, but not a special aptitude which children might possibly have and adults not. The study observed that there was little reason to accept the 'nimble fingers' argument either on the grounds of the adults' inability to work or their alleged lower pace of work. The study also contradicted the claim that the economics of match manufacture was such that the wages payable were low and could therefore only form part of the children's supplementary earnings. The report said that the piece-rate could not by itself show whether there was an economic advantage to the factory owners in employing children. The prevailing piece-rates were the equivalent of daily wage rates which were subtantially lower than even agricultural wages, yet women in large numbers were ready to work for these essentially child earnings. There might instead be non-economic gains in employing child workers who are outside the purview of labour legislation. Thus, docility might produce long-term economic gains in that children were more likely to execute unpaid work slipped between piece-rated jobs, and thefts of materials and wastage, which are elemental forms of protest, might be smaller.

Let us turn to Sivakasi in south India, which is the centre of the match industry. An ASS report (Banerjee, 1979) suggested that children constitute 40 to 45 per cent of the labour force in the industry, with between 20,000 to 28,000 children being employed. Girls outnumber boys by three to one and the minimum age of the children in the factories is five or six. Several decades ago most of the production was done at home on a piece-rate basis. Now, Sivakasi is dotted with factories and the factory owners recruit their labour in the surrounding villages. Child workers are herded into buses and transported to the factories. In 1979, 37 such children drowned en route to the factories when the bus carrying them got stuck in a flooded river. The Factories Act of 1948 fixes the minimum age for employment in India at 14 years. But there are many ways in which employers can circumvent official regulations, and even where the legal suppression of child work is successful the problem is shifted from the organized to the unorganized sector. Unregulated and unregistered factories have sprung up with poor children flocking into such unorganized industries as carpet manufacturing, wool cleaning, weaving, etc. For over 50 years, laws have existed in India against employing children in hazardous jobs. But there is no record of a single prosecution under them. One reason is the link between child-using factory owners and politicians, many of whom are in receipt of government subsidies. Many of these factory owners are former landowners who have made profits through the Green Revolution. They have become the land owners – many are themselves members of parliament, others fund politicians.

Indeed, the laws regarding child workers are frequently under review. There are some 12 items of legislation, which makes for a certain lack of uniformity. In fact, the government rejected a recommendation by its own Committee on Child Labour that the minimum age for employment of children should be 15, on the grounds that the time was not 'ripe' (ASS, 1984, p. 28). In 1986, the Concern for Working Children Group encouraged the Indian government to consider new legislation which would make all labour legal, but would attempt to control the number of hours worked and the kinds of jobs that children would be allowed to do. Gladins Kulothungan, a former member of the Concern for Working Children Group, supported this regularization of child labour, recognizing that the problem is unlikely to diminish significantly over the next three decades. The Group, in its draft proposal presented to the government, did not stipulate a minimum age realizing that, if that happened, at least one-third of child workers would be unprotected by the new legislation.

In 1986 there were indeed two major developments in India: the enactment of the Child Labour (Prohibition and Regulation) Act and the formulation of a National Policy on Child Labour. The

Girls searching for coal among the rubble, India
(*Source*: ILO)

thrust of government action consisted of three complementary measures. The Act firstly prohibits the employment of children below 14 in a hazardous occupation, and provides for a Child Labour Technical Advisory Committee to review and advise on hazardous occupations. In effect the Act sets out the priority areas for government action.

The second step involves the creation of a National Policy on Child Labour which anticipates the development of an extensive system of non-formal education. A target was set whereby all children who attain the age of 11 years by 1990 will have received five years of schooling (or its equivalent in non-formal education) and all children will by 1995 be provided with free and compulsory education up to the age of 14. The policy also anticipates the identification of employment and income-generating schemes in areas with a high incidence of child labour. In addition, the National Policy provides for specific pilot projects which are to establish the basis for a large national programme. These projects are to be implemented in ten areas and industries known to have a high incidence of child labour, as for instance in the match industry of Sivakasi. The strategy is to implement model programmes comprising a number of key elements including the promotion of general public awareness for: 'the role of programmes aimed at raising social awareness and changing attitudes cannot be minimized.'

Not only is the legislation radical in its own way, but so is the way in which the Concern for Working Children Group has used children themselves as advocates for the campaign to change the law. Using the medium of drama children have acted out real incidents, such as the loss of a hand by a 12-year-old boy who was working a machine meant only for skilled workers. These plays have been put on to video for national circulation. And in an episode reminiscent of the street children conference in Brazil, a play was put on in New Delhi at a conference of labour ministers. This is yet another persuasive argument for the role of children themselves in campaigning strategies for children's rights.

Perhaps the Indian authorities are being realistic in regularizing child work. As Guy Standing asserts, liberal legal instruments are excessively abstract and fail to attack specific cases of super-exploitation (Standing 1982, p. 614). Government legislation is to be expected, claims Standing, in the early phase of capitalist development, but with ironic unexpected effects. Firstly, it is likely to benefit those concerns most abusing child labour, for regulation will be more easily applied and accepted by the wage-paying formal sector because it is the more visible sector and the most subject to labour inspection. Ironically, it is those small-scale enterprises in the petty capitalist informal sector that are most likely to be using child labour and indulging in forms of super-exploitation, and which will be the least likely to be identified and subject to control. Indeed, such legislation will benefit those concerns most exploiting child workers; the cheapness of child labour could give them a competitive edge by which they could expand and possibly employ more child workers. The second irony is that such legislation may increase social inequality by reducing the income of poor families dependent upon the work contribution of their children.

Prohibiting child labour, then, seems paradoxically to make it harder to protect children. If child work is not allowed to exist in law, little can be done to improve it. Thus, child workers are automatically excluded from self-help organizations such as trade unions, which could improve their conditions of work. Perhaps the issue is not whether to legislate or not to legislate, but under what conditions regulations can be effective beyond the public relations, window-dressing level of government actions. According to Standing, '. . . legislation with effective bite will only be likely when child labour has actually become a marginal factor in the overall drive to capitalist accumulation' (Standing, 1982, p. 618). Standing quotes the example of Britain in the last century, where economic changes were already reducing the demand for child workers as the Education Acts and other legislation were coincidentally passed. Standing identifies forms of super-exploitation where the governments are likely to take ameliorative action if sufficiently pressed. It is those forms of child labour which are marginal, weakly supported and difficult for the government to legitimize. One example is pseudo-apprenticeship. As we have seen, these relationships are a typical means of circumventing minimum wage and other labour laws. If they were repeatedly exposed through critical research and political pressure, especially by trade unions, there might be grounds for optimism, given their marginal nature. However, one challenge is to develop the means to distinguish between real apprenticeship schemes and those which are fake. Another form of super-exploitation likely to be susceptible to pressure are those sub-contracting systems found in Morocco and elsewhere. They are a convenient system by which capitalists have made other groups perform a role they would otherwise have to undertake, that of controlling and disciplining the labour force. By virtue of their place in the labour process, these sub-contractors have no base of popular support. They are resented by the workers, and are tolerated, but not respected by middle classes. This lack of class support provides an opportunity for political action to register and categorize their activities as crucial steps towards their ultimate control and possible elimination, or at least to severely reducing their powers of exploitation. One might add the child domestic system to this list, dependent as it so often is on lifestyles whose underpinning values could be undermined by public education campaigns. The state is also more likely to be attracted to the street child phenomenon because of its high visibility and embarrassment factor. State action, though, may be of the palliative kind in which these children are swept off the street into institutions, as has happened periodically in Lima, Peru. Nevertheless, their very visibility does provide pressure groups with a powerful tool in any public awareness campaign aimed at exploring underlying socio-economic causes, and the advocacy of non-institutional programmes to meet their needs. It is to the construction of these campaigns that we must now turn.

6

Campaigning against Child Labour

Child labour is largely the product of poverty and underdevelopment and campaigning against it is not going to lead to its elimination overnight. Neither can the United Nations put the world to right by simply passing declarations and conventions in this field or any other. Action against child labour, if it is to be significant, must come from within states and be supported from outside. Campaigning, in the strict meaning of the word – a systematic attempt to arouse public opinion – is widely viewed as a necessary part of this process. After all, once a community reflects on the question of why children have to work and at what cost, the alternatives to child work point in the direction of those positive changes we call development. An attack on child labour is an attack on poverty and vice versa. And the first step is awareness raising of the individual, group and the society at large.

Campaigns are not new to the developing world. Both the Green Revolution in the 1960s and 1970s and the Universal Child Immunization Campaign of the 1980s are good examples of externally inspired development initiatives. In the latter case, UNICEF was able to inspire a massive immunization campaign in Colombia over the summer months of 1984. All media channels were utilized and some 120,000 volunteers were mobilized to achieve three-quarters coverage of the child population against five of the major childhood diseases. And the President fired the first shot in the campaign! (UNICEF, 1984, pp. 159–79) Columbia has inspired other examples of social mobilization behind child immunization. Could the same be achieved for child labour? One doubts it. Child immunization is self-evidently a good thing that most, if not all, governments find it in their interest to support. Not so with child labour, which is far more political in its implications.

The political sensitivity of child labour is reflected in the poor take-up of the chief international instrument in the field – ILO Convention 138. Few governments have ratified this convention which prohibits all work under 15 years. Many governments in the developing world find the instrument too ambitious given their economic reality. Indeed, many see child work in a family context as a naturally good thing – an expression of family solidarity. Besides, why should the state interfere with parental wishes? A clear echo here of nineteenth-century Britain. Not surprisingly, then, there is as yet no internationally orchestrated campaign against child labour, though the ILO has called for such systematic action at this level (Blanchard, 1983, p. 37). But there have been a number of international initiatives, and the potential does exist to construct more integrated programmes in support of government action, using in part lessons drawn from past campaigns. Let us now examine the main potential actors in such campaigns.

The ILO is widely viewed as the lead international agency concerned with child labour. Founded in 1919 as part of the League of Nations, it is now a unique agency within the United Nations system because of its tripartite representation of governments, employers' and workers' organizations. It is comparable to a ministry in a medium-sized country with a staff of 2,000. In a startling disclosure, its Director-General, Francis Blanchard, claimed that it consumed 22,000 pencils a year, 354 tonnes of paper and a million envelopes (*Guardian*, 15 August 1987). How many forests were destroyed on behalf of the child workers of the world must remain another little known development statistic! From the outset the ILO has attempted to regulate child labour in the short term without losing sight of the long-term goal of elimination. Its regulating and protective work has been expressed in terms of international standard setting. These international standards, or conventions, are only binding on those member states who ratify them. Once ratified, article 22 of the ILO's Constitution requires signatories to provide annual reports on their compliance, while articles 24 and 26 allow for the consideration of complaints against a state for failure to live up to the instrument in question. Perhaps an additional reason for a lack of enthusiasm for Convention 138.

The first child work convention was passed in 1919, setting the minimum age for regular industrial work, excluding family enterprise and technical schools, at 14. This Convention no. 5 was revised in 1937 when the minimum age was raised to 15.

From 1920 to 1965 minimum age conventions were adopted for the areas shown in table 6.1.

Table 6.1 ILO minimum age conventions, 1920–65

Occupation	Convention	Minimum age
Seamen	No. 7 1920	14
	No. 58 1936	15
Agriculture	No. 10 1921	14 (except out of school hours)
Mining	No. 123 1965	16
Non-industrial	No. 33 1932	14 (but allows children over 12 to be employed outside of school hours on light work)

ILO conventions are usually flexible, allowing for gradual implementation and the facility for a state to grant exceptions (so called 'saving clauses'), particularly in the case of family enterprises. In 1973 the ILO replaced these conventions with Convention 138 which applies to all areas of economic activity. Convention 138, coupled with Recommendation 146, is the most comprehensive international instrument and statement on child labour:

Convention 138
CONVENTION CONCERNING MINIMUM AGE FOR ADMISSION TO EMPLOYMENT

Article 1
Each Member for which this Convention is in force undertakes to pursue a national policy designed to ensure the effective abolition of child labour and to raise progressively the minimum age for admission to employment or work to a level

consistent with the fullest physical and mental development of young persons.

Article 2

3   The minimum age specified in pursuance of paragraph 1 of this Article shall not be less than the age of completion of compulsory schooling and, in any case, shall not be less than 15 years.

Article 3

1   The minimum age for admission to any type of employment or work which by its nature or the circumstances in which it is carried out is likely to jeopardise the health, safety or morals of young persons shall not be less than 18.

Recommendation No. 146

i National Policy
   . . . high priority should be given to planning for and meeting the needs of children and youth in national development policies and programmes . . .
ii Minimum Age 7(1)
   Members should take as their objective the progressive raising to 16 years of the minimum age for admission to employment or work specified in pursuance of Article 2 of the Minimum Age Convention 1973.

As with previous conventions, no. 138 contains flexible provisions and saving clauses. The ratification of Convention 138 has been disappointing. By 1979 only 13 countries had ratified it and by 1988 this figure had risen to 36.

There are those, like the UK delegate to the UN Seminar, who assert that this paltry number overstates support for Convention 138. It was Professor Boudhiba who pointed out in his report that states often seemed to ratify conventions without having the means to implement them. So, as the UK delegate asserted, what is the point of ratifying conventions one cannot implement, and then hectoring others for not doing so? At the Seminar, The Netherlands took a different view, asserting that ratification of such instruments is an indication of the political will to broadly comply with their provisions, and that it was necessary to show support for the principles they embody.

Whether for or against, all that states need do as members of the ILO is to bring conventions to the attention of their relevant authorities. In the case of no. 138, the UK Government did so in 1974 by publishing a White Paper setting out general support for the convention but claiming that it could not ratify it as yet. This has remained the official UK position ever since. Indeed the UK delegate to the UN Seminar stated that UK regulations on child work complied with, if not exceeded, the provisions of Convention 138. So why not ratify? Perhaps the most telling argument against is the reporting provision – why have your country held up to international scrutiny if you can avoid it?

Nevertheless, the ILO finds consolation in the fact that most member states have adopted a minimum age standard of 14 or higher, although a smaller group of countries have set the minimum age at between 12 and 13. Additionally, more than 100 countries have ratified one or more of the ten conventions prior to 1973. These conventions regulate industrial employment and dangerous work much more rigorously than family enterprise and agriculture.

The ILO has hardly been zealous in following up on Convention 138. IYC (1979) provided the first real opportunity for the ILO and other agencies to focus world attention on the issue of child labour. In his declaration concerning IYC, the Director-General stated that:

(a) a child is not a 'small adult' but a person entitled to self-fulfilment through learning and play so that his adult life is not jeopardized by his having to work at an early age;

(b) governments should ... take all necessary social and legislative action for the progressive elimination of child labour;

(c) pending the elimination of child labour, it must be regulated and humanized.

A number of important publications emerged from the IYC, but the ILO's attention did not become re-focused on the issue until 1983, when the Director-General's Report made a special feature of child labour. The reality behind the exhortation has meant that the ILO has not been able to obtain major donor support for its child labour activities. This state of affairs was openly pointed to by an ILO delegate to the UN Seminar who virtually pleaded with the government delegates to reverse the low priority given to the issue by member states. Understandably, then, the sensitivity with which governments view child labour has encouraged a cautious approach by the ILO. Despite its tripartite structure, it is governments who really count. They pay the bills and they count for more in difficult economic times.

There were NGO observers at the UN Seminar who held that UNICEF ought to be the principal agency for child labour because of its specific responsibility for child welfare. In looking ahead to the adoption of a UN Convention on the Rights of the Child, some NGOs saw UNICEF as the chief regulatory agency for this instrument. Despite these lofty ambitions (flattering in one sense, but utterly naïve) the political realities facing UNICEF are no less constraining, while its operating budget is less than that of Hampshire County Council in Britain. UNICEF, unlike ILO, was established in 1946 on a voluntary basis. It began as a temporary relief operation mainly in Europe, and it was not until 1953 that its mandate to work exclusively in the developing world became firmly established. Each year UNICEF has to go to governments for support, and in particular to the US government, its largest donor. This economic reality may account for the public relations style and strategy adopted by UNICEF's Executive Director from 1982. Under James Grant, UNICEF has made the Child Survival and Development Revolution (CSDR) its main campaigning thrust. CSDR refers to a package of low-cost child health measures which UNICEF claims could halve infant mortality rates if adopted world-wide. Emphasis on CSDR, and latterly on the universal immunization goal for 1990, tends to obscure the more broadly-based development work UNICEF continues to support.

Nevertheless, at its 1984 Executive Board, UNICEF was asked, mainly at the insistence of its Scandinavian members, to review its policy on Children in Especially Difficult Circumstances. This reflected a concern that UNICEF was neglecting important child development issues in its emphasis on child survival. The report presented to UNICEF's 1986 Executive Board covered a review of working and street children; children in armed conflict and in situations of natural disaster; and those subject to abuse. The final draft paper observed:

> UNICEF, within the context of existing programmes of support and in co-operation with other agencies, should advocate and

support the progressive abolition of child exploitation, the protection of working children and street children, the amelioration of working conditions and the analysis of the impact of national policies on these children. While the underlying causes are basically structural – widespread poverty, underdevelopment and gross inequality – society must do more than wait for the long-term results of structural changes that it may be seeking to effect. Through extending the child survival and development strategy in response to the special needs of these children and youth, families and communities can be strengthened to decrease and/or prevent the exploitation of child work and the growth of numbers of street children. (UNICEF, 1986a, p. 11)

In a rather confused final debate, what emerged was the recognition that UNICEF should play a major role within the UN system for street children, but in terms of actions should, 'concentrate mainly on advocacy and rely primarily on governments and voluntary agencies for implementation' (UNICEF, 1986d, p. 3). Advocacy was therefore seen as UNICEF's natural role and advantage while the more sensitive campaigning work should be left to NGOs. On the funding side, the expansion of programmes would have to be left to the initiative of field offices and secure supplementary funding for 'noted projects' (projects funded not out of UNICEF's mainstream budget, but by National Committees).

The outcome of the 1986 Board was more positive than many had hoped. It was a flexible and realistic response to the situation facing UNICEF. In the child labour field, UNICEF's intention was to build on what it knew best, i.e., non-institutional programmes for street children, and gradually extending the lessons of Latin America to the new challenges of Africa and Asia. The emphasis on the 'noted projects' mechanism again builds on past policy. Some $2 million was raised in this way in the early 1980s, with only a small $500,000 commitment from UNICEF's stretched general resources. But will UNICEF campaign against child labour? Given the realities of a threatened annual budget of some $400 mmillion which UNICEF has to raise each year, campaigning is too politically sensitive to contemplate. Child Survival brings in the money while UNICEF quietly goes on with its broad-based field programmes.

Many see child labour as a human rights issue so, finally, it is worth pointing to a number of United Nations pronouncements on human rights which relate to child labour:

1   The Universal Declaration of Human Rights, 1948.
2   The International Covenant on Human Rights, 1966.
3   The Supplementary Convention on the Abolition of Slavery, 1956.
4   The Convention for the Suppression of the Traffic in Persons and of the Exploitation of the Prostitution of Others, 1949.
5   The Declaration of the Rights of the Child, 1959.

Additionally, regional organizations such as the Council of Europe, the Organization of African Unity and the Organization of American States, have their own instruments.

Since the International Year of the Child, NGOs have become an increasingly powerful force, lobbying the UN system to adhere to the principles enshrined in these instruments, and to take more effective action against child labour. NGOs like the Anti-Slavery Society, have produced some of the best documented country studies of child labour. Others, like the Geneva-based Defence for Children International have taken up the human rights dimension of child labour and effectively lobbied UN agencies (particularly UNICEF) to pay more attention to the issue.

But of all the NGOs, it is perhaps the trade unions who have the greatest untapped potential for action, both at the national and international level. The Trades Union Congress of Britain produced its own educational resource on child labour in 1985, and subsequently lobbied the ILO Governing Body to follow this example by doing more in the field of public education (see Fyfe, 1985). In *Breaking Down the Wall of Silence* the ICFTU resolved that 'free trade unions all over the world will pave the way for the eventual abolition of child labour' (ICFTU, 1986, p. 34). But the same organization faces its own constraints in acting upon this commitment. Its resources are limited and have only permitted small-scale projects, such as a vocational education initiative in Bombay. More fundamental, though, is the reality that many of its developing world affiliates are lukewarm at best, given their members' dependence on child work. The ICFTU has, therefore, gone along with the humanizing strategy, which the TUC has often opposed, of ameliorative actions which deliver services, like health and education, to the child at work, or attempts at loosening the rigidities of the school system so that working children can fit education around their work schedule.

These pragmatic projects and programmes recognize the need for children to work. But to change that reality, to eliminate the necessity for children to work, is a radical shift which requires a long-term integrated international effort, and virtually everyone agrees that public education campaigns are the first necessary, but not sufficient, steps along a very long road. The Report of the Director-General of the ILO in 1983 provides the essential rationale:

> The role of information gathering and dissemination in raising public awareness of the evils of child labour and in exposing the sectors of activities where it is prevalent should not be under-estimated. In many developing countries there is a surprisingly high degree of ignorance about the consequences of child labour in general and the ill-effects of unsafe working conditions in particular. Child work is often accepted as part of the natural state of things, and the rights and needs of the child are not always fully appreciated. A great deal of effort, therefore, needs to be made to generate and promote public awareness of the consequences of child labour and the rights of the working child and to expose unacceptable conditions wherever they exist. (Blanchard, 1983, p. 23).

The Anti-Slavery Society in a report commissioned by UNICEF as part of its preparation for the 1986 Executive Board suggested that, 'Trends in the use of child labour could be reversed by public education on the needs and the rights of children' (ASS, 1984b, p. 49). The trade union movement has an enormous potential role to play in this area. As Professor Boudhiba has pointed out: 'the unions . . . would still seem not to be clearly aware of the magnitude of the question. They should be requested to include specific activity on this matter in their programmes. They are active pressure groups that can have a decisive effect on governments, employers, enterprises and public opinion' (Boudhiba, 1982, p. 71).

The ICFTU in recognizing the need to respond to the challenge of child labour, and in its own report to its members early in 1986, observed that: '. . . public opinion was largely ignorant of the problem and must be made aware of the dangers of child labour, the damage it can cause to family life and to entire societies and economies.' UNICEF's Draft Working Paper for its 1986 Executive Board recommended that UNICEF should work to enhance government and public awareness of children in especially difficult circumstances and of possibilities for preventive and ameliorative actions (UNICEF, 1986a, p. 14). Finally, the UN Seminar on Child Labour called on governmental, international and non-governmental organizations '. . . to increase awareness amongst children, parents, workers and employers of the causes and the adverse effects of child labour and the measures to combat its exploitation' (UN, 1986, p. 28).

If everyone is agreed that the raising of public awareness is the first essential step in the child labour campaign, there is little in the way of guidance on how best this can be done. Perhaps the past is our only guide. The question of whether it is possible to derive lessons from the past has, of course, long exercised historians. Many historians would now claim that this is a futile endeavour; however, for the student of child labour campaigns, the past is virtually the only reference point. And as long as one avoids attempts at drawing crude parallels between nineteenth-century Britain and the contemporary developing world, the past can provide important pointers for those wishing to conceptualize, and contruct, child labour campaigns.

The first campaigns against child labour took place in Britain just over 200 years ago over the issue of child chimney sweeps. Prior to the 1780s, child work was taken for granted in Britain and Europe. It was philanthropists like Jonas Hanway who turned child labour into a public issue. Hanway's aim, like those of the early nineteenth-century philanthropists, was not to abolish child labour but to regulate it through parliamentary action. Then, in 1803, with the foundation of the Society for Superseeding the Necessity of Climbing Boys we witness the first attempt to abolish a form of child labour. According to Hugh Cunningham, the early reformers had to overcome four major obstacles (Cunningham, 1985, p. 1). There was, firstly, the traditional assumption that it was natural for children to work and to contribute to the family economy. Secondly, that the problem was too little work for children rather than too much. Thirdly, a belief that parents had the right to do what they wished with their children, and finally the *laissez-faire* belief in the value of free labour. That these obstacles were gradually surmounted is now part of the romantic story of child labour in nineteenth-century Britain – a romance which has stuck in English history textbooks for over 50 years and become as universal as the story of 1066.

What was the reality of these first campaigns and what lessons can be learnt from them? It is a long story, for it is only gradually that we witness in nineteenth-century Britain an awakening of social conscience. Then in the latter half of the century 'a veritable fury of compassion' (Thompson, 1984, p. 384) produced 'an extreme sensibility to human suffering' (Bagehot in Collins, 1965, pp. 178–9). But how was this transformation achieved? The movement to protect children from the new impersonal and systematic exploitation under industrial capitalism took over a century to achieve its goal. This campaign was never broadly based, comprising as it did a handful of enlightened professional men from the industrial north, the workers' own Short-Time Committees, and the parliamentary skills of Lord Shaftesbury. At the centre of the campaign was the task of building the evidence which proved so effective in persuading the nation of the iniquities of child labour. The first step was the raising of awareness; many people were simply unaware of the conditions of child work around them. Richard Oastler, who became one of the leading factory reformers, had to be told about child labour abuse even though he lived alongside it. As E. P. Thompson observes, 'we forget how long abuses can continue unknown until they are articulated; how people can look at misery and not notice it, until misery itself rebels' (Thompson, 1984, p. 377).

Oastler founded the Short-Time Committees which collected evidence for the Parliamentary Committees. These in turn allowed working people to speak for themselves about the abuses of child labour. The children themselves gave testimony, particularly to the Royal Commission which in 1842 examined women's and children's work in the mines. A public accustomed to the horror stories of factory work was unprepared for the stories of child miners of seven working 14 hours a day in conditions that disabled and deformed them. Victorians were particularly susceptible to accounts of sexual depravity and exploitation, which working naked down the mines encouraged – it was this more than any other feature which shocked contemporary opinion.

For the Victorians it was the potential for sexual exploitation in the expanding industries which moved them into action. The Mines Act of 1842 was passed virtually overnight. In the end it was not factory legislation, but free compulsory education, which proved the most effective child labour law. The campaign for universal schooling was much more popularly based and culminated in the passing of the Education Act of 1870. This act expressed both a changing view of childhood and the belief that the future of the nation was ultimately served best not by making children work, but by educating them.

We must examine the techniques used by the Victorian campaigners which gradually took children out of the workplace and deposited them in the classroom, and we can identify key elements in the process which altogether provide a model for contemporary campaigns. The Victorian campaign was built firstly upon detailed *investigation*, which was of two kinds: leading figures in the campaign, like Shaftesbury, had to brief themselves and raise their own awareness; then, there were the institutional investigations of the Select Committees and the Royal Commissions. Any investigation necessarily leads to *analysis*: in the case of child labour new social investigators like Henry Mayhew were helping to provide a classification of child workers for the first time. After analysis comes the need for *public exposure*, as the first step in raising public awareness: the 1830s and 1840s in Britain became the era of the great extra-parliamentary pressure groups; the factory movement drew much inspiration from the Anti-Slavery Movement, the most powerful and effective of these in publicizing its cause. It was vital that the new knowledge of the factory conditions be *disseminated* widely. Robert Owen, the enlightened factory owner and model paternalist (it was Owen who established the first pre-school in Britain at his New Lanark factory in 1816), clearly recognized this, believing as he did in 'the multiplication of reason by means of its diffusion.'

To move a mass audience needs a transformation of abstract notions into a medium more concrete and emotional in its appeal. Significantly, Hanway, the first campaigner, called his book on child chimney sweeps, *A Sentimental History* (1785) in a deliberate attempt to engage the emotions of the public. Climbing boys were tailor-made for the early campaigners because of their high visibility (unlike factory children and child miners they entered the homes of the wealthy) and because their appearance and recruitment facilitated the slave/savage analogy; when the slave analogy was extended to factory children it became a powerful emotional tool (Cunningham, 1985, p. 2). Popular writers like Charles Dickens and Charles Kingsley transformed the new knowledge into a fictional form with which a mass audience could identify. Dickens could equally lay claim to the title of the 'children's champion' of Victorian Britain. His child heroes, from Little Nell (1840) to Jo in *Bleak House* (1853), presented for the first time the child's world from within. *Bleak House* in particular became proverbial and even the 'street arabs' treasured such tattered copies of the instalments as they could lay their hands on. Dickens's vast international appeal was instrumental in assisting both the factory reformers and more particularly the campaigners for universal free schooling.

The factory movement was able to utilize the remarkable pockets of literacy within the working class. It was workers' groups who established 'reading societies' to buy the new radical newspapers, such as the *Poor Man's Advocate* and the *Voice of the People*. The movement also produced its first pamphlets in 1836, and even the illiterate were not excluded from political discourse. Ballad singers and 'patteres' presented current political issues through song and theatre, and workers would walk miles to hear a radical speaker. The growing power of newpspaers is graphically revealed by the case of W. T. Stead's account in the *Pall Mall Gazette* of buying a 13-year-old prostitute. This produced such a public clamour that it brought swift parliamentary action in 1885 to raise the age of consent and curb child prostitution. Contrast this with the painstaking efforts of Josephine Butler and others throughout the 1860s and 1870s to expose the 'white slave trade' which had consistently been ignored.

Such new opportunities for the *dissemination* of information fed into the consequent activities of *mobilization* and *pressure* for *action*. These campaigns for political action did not always succeed (parliamentary inquiries were often as not a means of diffusing discontent), but from the *evaluation* of the points of resistance a new dissemination campaign could be mounted with a fresh attempt at mobilization.

Out of the historically important experience of Victorian Britain, we can now construct a Child Labour Campaign Model, as in figure 6.1.

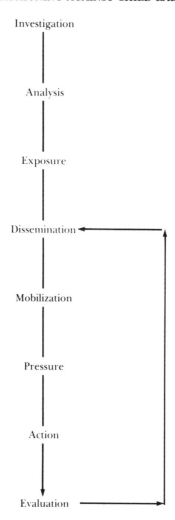

Figure 6.1   The child labour campaign model

1 *Investigation*: This is the first step of acquiring information through research by mass media, NGOs, trade unions, universities, government agencies, international agencies.

2 *Analysis*: The information needs processing to arrive at plausible explanations concerning causes, consequences and measures to be taken.

3 *Exposure*: Such interpretations need a public airing through publications, etc.

4 *Dissemination*: Wider dissemination is then needed via the mass media, trade union education structures, etc., to generate greater public awareness.

5 *Mobilization*: of those groups most likely to act, such as trade unions, NGOs, churches, etc.

6 *Pressure*: Through campaigns pressure is put on the authorities to act to eradicate the worst abuses of child labour and to protect and improve the welfare of child workers in line with internationally agreed standards.

7 *Action*: Positive action which can be anticipated would include adoption of ILO standards, better labour inspection, punitive measures against employers guilty of the worst practices, improved provision of health, welfare and educational services for those children most at risk.

8 *Evaluation*: All action needs evaluation, especially if, as is often the case, it is not successful the first time. Once you find out what went wrong with the campaign, you can marshal new information and 'loop back' again with a fresh attempt at dissemination and mobilization.

Though all the elements of the models were present in the Victorian child labour campaign, they were not applied continuously either by individuals or pressure groups. Trade unions, which potentially could have activated the model fully, had not yet developed a mass membership, and therefore the capacity for action, until after the Education Acts sealed the fate of child labour. Dickens, though a genius at popular dissemination, never significantly involved himself in political mobilization; while Shaftesbury, an expert in parliamentary pressure, kept himself aloof from popular movements.

When we look at the developing world today we see all manner of possibilities for integrated public awareness campaigns which would have been beyond the capability of those in the last century. To begin with, we only need to look at the means of mass communication available in developing countries. Perhaps for the first time large areas of the developing world have the organization and communication structure to inform and support the majority to bring about change. Twenty years ago radios were a rarity. Today there are 8,000 radio stations in the developing world broadcasting to over one billion transistors. Twenty years ago the print media was relatively underdeveloped. Today there are 8,000 daily newspapers in the developing world. Television is also a growing force, reaching as it does some 50–60 per cent of the urban population. India has had a decade of experimentation with satellite TV to promote village education, and by 1990 almost three-quarters of its 670 million population will have access to TV. Such developments provide enormous scope for non-formal education, training and information dissemination. A number of campaigns already bear witness to this, from the spread of the Green Revolution to attempts to promote family planning, child health and adult literacy.

Equally, one can point to the educational opportunities provided by the remarkable expansion in schooling in the developing world during the 1960s and 1970s. By 1981, countries such as Sri Lanka, Tanzania, Kenya and Vietnam were achieving 100 per cent primary school enrolments. Today 80 per cent of all children are enrolled in formal education, making the school system one of the most important channels of communication for the vast majority of today's and tomorrow's parents. Nevertheless, this expansion masks fundamental defects. There are still major inequalities of access between urban and rural areas, and boys and girls. Drop-out rates continue to be universally high – up to 70 per cent in some cases. The absolute numbers not in school continue to rise with high birth-rates (110 million in 1960, rising to 121 million in 1975). What is also disturbing is the decline in educational expenditure (16.4 per cent of total government expenditure in 1982, reduced to 5.9 per cent in 1981) with the global recession. Despite this, primary schools, in particular, remain an important tool in any public awareness campaign against child labour as, for example, in the possibility of building child-to-child alliances.

The Green Revolution and child immunization campaigns have shown that there is no substitute for the political will to mobilize all the possible channels of communication. Political leadership was vital in the promotion of the Green Revolution and Family Planning in Indonesia, and for the remarkable success of the Child Immunization Campaign in Colombia in 1984. Equally significant is the growth of non-governmental organizations. India alone has 12,000 voluntary organizations and Bangladesh 6,000. Specifically, one can point to the growth of organized religion as a major development resource. Trade unionism, too, is on the increase in much of the developing world, albeit from a low base, and in the last decade there has been the growth of the Women's Movement. Additionally, one can mention the growth of the major youth movements of the Boy Scouts (16 million members world-wide) and Girl Guides (8 millon members world-wide). To these indigenous NGOs should be added the over 3,000 NGOs in industrial countries, such as Radda Barnen and OXFAM, who are significant partners in grassroots development.

If the potential change agents and the tools for social mobilization are in place, how can they be used in the campaign against child labour? This is the most difficult task of all because in a world where information technology has become the new wonder of the age, shamefully little is known about how to communicate information whose principal value is to the poor. Nevertheless, there are a number of initiatives which are indicative of how the Child Labour Campaign Model might operate in practice. In Kenya there is the recent WHO-sponsored Child Labour and Health Project, run by Dr Philista Onyango of the University of Nairobi. The project team engaged during 1984–5 in a number of activities which mirror the model. Beginning with an investigation in eight districts in Nairobi they analysed the data and disseminated it through workshops and seminars. The project's dissemination strategy was initially aimed at parents and employers and, given the problem of illiteracy, they significantly used the medium of community drama. The team considered drama as perhaps the most powerful tool for not only presenting issues like child labour, but as a tool for collective problem analysis (Dr Philista Onyango). The rationale behind the use of drama was its capacity both to hold the interest of large groups of parents and employers through entertainment, and to create awareness of the dangerous aspects of child labour. It was seen as vital that the people participated in this exercise through role play as part of the process of identifying the problem. This was followed by discussion out of which emerged suggested solutions. This is a good example of active learning which appears to have led to attitude shifts regarding the value of rural to urban migration (Onyango, 1986, p. 169).

The research activities of the team identified four groups which needed to be mobilized: the parents (producers), the employers (consumers), the children (products) and the decision makers. Out of these the 'producers' and 'consumers' were the least likely to perceive child labour as exploitative because they benefited from it,

Community theatre group performing in a shanty town, Lima,
Peru
(*Source*: Mauricio Audibert)

while the official view was that child labour law was effective and the
problem did not exist. As the research team had identified child
workers as school drop-outs, they decided to take school children as
their target audience in the next phase. Out of this evaluation the
team 'looped back' in the model to a new dissemination strategy to
ensure that every effort was made to reduce the high drop-out rate
from primary schools. For despite the introduction of free primary
education in 1974, five years later of the original 63 per cent of girls
and boys enrolled in standard 1, only 14.76 per cent of girls and

13.85 per cent of boys were enrolled in standard 5. The project in its next phase intends to use drama in schools to create awareness of the opportunity cost of leaving school at an early stage, particularly in terms of adult employment prospects, and to try to involve children themselves in suggesting possible solutions.

In Peru, an NGO coalition co-ordinated by TIPACOM (Talleres Infantiles Proyectados a la Comunidad) has, since the early 1980s, mounted a Children's Rights Campaign mainly in the shanty-towns of Lima. Community participation was central to the strategy of creating awareness and mobilizing people for action. In the shanty-town district of 3 de Mayo a Committee for the Defence of the Rights of the Child (CODEM) has been constituted by the parents and there is a similar children's committee. The aim of the committees is to investigate children's problems and to formulate possible solutions. The Committee of NGOs working in this all-year-round campaign has found direct communication through audio-visual presentations and drama the most effective channels of communication. Now, CODEM is producing its own newsletter. Though TV and radio were thought too costly by the Children's Rights Campaign, it is worth a small digression to point to the value of popular radio for the rural areas of Peru, and by extension to Latin America and the developing world. Radio is the medium best suited to the rural areas of Peru since it is both cheap and well adapted to the oral tradition of the peasantry. Recent experiments in educational radio are particularly noteworthy, such as *Tierra Fecunda* (Fertile Land) first broadcast in 1983. It has proved popular in disseminating a wide range of information not simply confined to agricultural practice. The impact achieved by *Tierra Fecunda* is evidenced by a network of over 700 correspondents throughout the country who receive 300 letters a month and about 3,000 correspondents bringing information and materials. This and similar radio programmes throughout the developing world represent an important delivery system which could be put at the disposal of the Child Labour Campaign.

The Centre of Concern for Child Labour in Bangkok, Thailand, is a good example of an integrated approach to the raising of public awareness. Established in 1981 by an ecumenical association of Buddhists, Catholics and Protestants, the Centre operates across the activities of research, dissemination, pressure and welfare services provision. In 1982, the Centre published pamphlets containing warnings and advice for those rural families, especially in the impoverished north-east of the country, who are forced each year to send their children to work in Bangkok. The pamphlets were disseminated on a large scale to governors and governmental agencies for eventual distribution among villagers, labour officials and the media. In 1983 the Centre conducted research in Vierirem Province collecting information on children who had disappeared after obtaining work in Bangkok factories.

These grassroots organizations originating small-scale projects in the public education field often work in isolation. There is a clear need not only to learn and, where possible, generalize from their experiences, but also to network them so that they can learn from each other. What these innovative projects generally have in common is a commitment to community participation which owes a great deal to the seminal work of the Brazilian educationalist Paulo Freire. In the early 1960s, Freire pioneered a new method of working with adult illiterates in his native north-east of Brazil. At the heart of this methodology is the concept of 'conscientization' – the awakening of a critical consciousness in poor people. For Freire the way to break the 'culture of silence' characteristic of poor communities is through non-formal education. Indeed, Dickens's severe schoolmaster, Mr Gradgrind's obsession with facts, epitomizes what Friere terms the 'banking concept of education', the aim of which is to fill people's minds with the facts and ideas of others. But to promote real awareness one needs to encourage people to think for themselves – to involve them in 'problem-posing education'. The co-ordinators of such programmes of education motivate through the use of the problems of poor people. These topics are typically raised in discussion groups or 'culture circles' using visual media like slides or pictures. Freire's ideas were highly influential in the 1970s but are essentially only a restatement of a precept as old as education itself: that people learn best by finding out for themselves. It was Pascal who observed that: '. . . we are usually convinced more easily by reasons we have found ourselves than by those which have occurred to others.' Freire's methodology is important because of the principles of community involvement, and starting from where people are and are not from where you wish to take them. One could envisage 'learning circles' in which a discussion starter was: 'Is it better for our children to work rather than to go to school?'

These innovative projects are highly indicative of the types of techniques and strategies which might be further elaborated. What is needed now is a move beyond these fragmentary initiatives to a more systematic and integrated global strategy. In such a strategy one can identify at least three major action programmes. They are *workshops*, *training manuals*, and *mass communication campaigns*. Regional and national workshops are an important activity to enable people on the ground to share experiences and ideas. If participants are carefully selected, they offer an opportunity for identifying priorities and setting an agenda of feasible actions. They also provide the elements of a future network which is vital if the learning process is to be developed. Regional workshops to encompass the Americas, Africa, and Asia would need to have representatives of governments and workers' and employers' associations. The involvement of teacher unions should be particularly encouraged, given that they straddle both the world of child welfare and organized labour. In nineteenth and early twentieth-century Britain, teacher unions were an important factor in ensuring that poor children remained in school and had access to health and welfare services. Out of these well-prepared regional meetings it is important that a future agenda of regular reporting back on national experience is built in. Any programme of national workshops ought again to retain this basic tripartite core, added to which could be relevant NGOs, health professionals, the mass media and lawyers. The latter would seem to be another neglected professional group. Lawyers have a vested interest in child labour law, but they themselves may need educating first. As Jeremy Bentham pointed out: 'Lawyers are the only persons in whom the ignorance of the law is not punished.' Again, the basic aim would be to generate a deeper awareness of the problem with the objective of working towards the constitution of a national coalition for action. Perhaps these might be designated 'Child Protection Alliances' with a prominent patron. The CLC (Child Labour Campaign) Model outlined in this book would offer a practical tool for conceptualizing the design of public awareness campaigns, either at the macro level of a nationally co-ordinated movement, or at the micro level of NGOs, workers' or employers' action. The field testing of the model at both levels would be vital and the experiences of its use, with suggestions for modifications, could be shared at regular regional meetings.

The next step must be an examination of the tools for action at the community level. Here the development of training manuals, particularly, but not exclusively, for trade unions, needs exploring. Historically trade unions have not played a major role in the campaign against child labour and they continue to treat the issue as a low priority. This limited interest can and ought to be reversed through workers' education programmes, which would generate awareness of the implications of child labour for the health and development of children, their future capacity as adult workers, and its negative effects on income distribution and employment. Greater awareness of international conventions, national laws and regulations is another precondition for enhancing the capacity of workers' associations to put greater pressure on governments for action. Workers' associations do have the potential for mounting the type of integrated campaigns envisaged by the CLC model. They can play an important role in the detection and identification of child labour abuse. Through their own educational structures they can analyse this data, and then design campaigns using dissemination strategies that educate and mobilize, not only their own grassroots membership but also the general public. Workers' associations have an important role to play in organizing the unorganized, especially in the informal urban sector where so much child labour is concentrated. The extension of workers' solidarity to these marginal workers and communities would, in turn, facilitate the more effective dissemination of information and knowledge, thereby opening up new possibilities in popular participation for change.

Training manuals for the literate trade union activist would make a significant contribution to the methodology of organizing workers' education on a more informal and flexible basis at the community level. Such manuals would essentially be resources for tutors working with small groups of activists in workshop settings. They would function both as a resource and as a guide for people who would later run their own education programmes at the community level. As an exemplar the manual could offer a guide to co-operative learning. Active learning exercises built into manuals could increase participants' understanding of the issue of child labour, and their campaigning skills would be developed through the use and application of the CLC model.

The Trade Union Congress has already developed such a manual on child labour for its own membership (see Fyfe, 1985). The Commonwealth Trade Union Council has, through its technical co-operation programme, particularly in Africa, experience of using training manuals and preparing 'study circle' books. One can envisage the adoption of a similar methodology with other appropriate groups. The use of manuals in teacher training is a clear possibility to develop teachers' child welfare capacity, and to enable them to improve curricula so that schoolchildren themselves can be mobilized in the campaign. Schools not only need a more relevant curriculum in order to retain children, they also need more flexible working arrangements to fit in with the needs of working children. In Peru, a national orgnization of working children called MANTHOC, established since 1977, has attempted to create such awareness within the teaching profession. Employers, too, could be reached through an appeal to enlightened self-interest, as it would help erode cheap labour competition. Many employers in the small-scale and marginal sector might be willing to comply with the law if they were aware of the regulations and the penalties of non-compliance. Besides, employers could be appealed to in terms of the delivery of health services to child workers. Robert Owen used the argument with other employers that it was just as important to maintain human capital as physical capital if productivity was to be maximized. Both the WHO and ILO recognize that it is possible to influence employers. There is little doubt too that a training manual resource would be an important tool for a range of NGOs to develop their advocacy function. After all, training manuals provide the stimulus by which people educate themselves and develop their organizational skills.

Resource development to facilitate the mass dissemination of information and to promote awareness is the third and final element in the integrated action programme. What can be done here to reach the mass of ordinary people, in particular parents? We must look to the mass communications media, particularly TV and radio, as powerful tools of social marketing. Again there are models to act as guides in the use of the mass media for public education. The ILO in 1985 began a mass media campaign in Latin America using a series of TV spots (of 15–30 seconds duration) to promote the message of equal rights for women. The ILO has been able to obtain the agreement of governments, workers and employers to this programme, and the national TV agreed to open up prime-time slots for these 'commercials'. The TV slots use a variety of media, including cartoons, to convey messages concerning equal rights for women. The series includes 12 TV spots which are repeated for 2–3 weeks before changing to the next. Argentina was the first to adopt the package in November 1985, followed by Bolivia, and similar agreements have been signed with the majority of the countries in the Americas Region. There is little doubt that such an approach would work equally well in urban areas to deliver messages on the dangerous effects of child work, and particularly as a means of reaching those 'invisible' child workers who are employed as domestics in middle-class homes. It may well be that child domestic work (a priority concern in the field) is the most susceptible to this kind of public education campaign as so much of it rests on the attitudes and lifestyles of a group of affluent people who, unlike employers, have no collective strength.

But what of the rural areas? Here, radio takes over, and we have already seen examples of attempts to use popular radio for development purposes. There is no reason to believe that programmes could not be devised, which, rather than castigating poor people for making their children work (for of course there are exploitative parents), communicated messages concerning the health and learning needs of children and how they could organize to press for improved services. Slide-tape presentations might also be used in village meetings. Already a group of Asian NGOs, collectively called Child Workers in Asia Support Group have used sets of slides based on a comic telling the story of a child worker from India. In addition, there is a cassette, a script, a copy of the comic, a set of eight pictures and a guide on how to organize group meetings. Any audio-visual package ought to be supported by such a group leader's guide. This proposed programme of integrated activities should not simply be a 'top-down' process. A 'bottom-up' feedback mechanism, in which lessons at the grassroots level are fed in at the national, regional and global levels, is vital if we are to improve the art of public awareness raising in relation to the child labour problem. It is the international agencies like ILO, UNICEF and WHO who are best placed to sponsor the piloting of such an integrated programme in public education, but it will still be left to governments to engage in full-scale implementation.

7

Debates and Dilemmas

> The biggest mistake was made by he who did nothing because he could
> only do a little.
>
> Edmund Burke

In this final chapter I shall begin by summing up the current
situation of child labour as a public policy issue before exploring the
ethical dilemmas the problem still raises. In developed countries,
universal primary education is fully achieved and secondary
education is virtually attained. However, there are many instances,
even in the most advanced industrialized countries, of large
numbers of children engaged in work sometimes of a super-
explotative nature, as in the case of child prostitution and pornography. In this area countries like the USA and The Netherlands are
world leaders in a multi-billion dollar industry in which children are
bought and sold (see 1984 DCI Report on a Child Auction in
Amsterdam, *International Children's Rights Monitor*, vol. 2/1, 1985,
pp. 10–15). This should chasten all those in industrialized countries
who state that child labour has been consigned to the scrap heap of
history. Sexual exploitation is clearly an extreme case and the principal problem is one of inadequate protection for children under
existing legislation. Then there is the more general problem of children who combine work with schooling, and the tendency for certain sectors (for example, agriculture) to be exempt from child
labour regulations, either because work in such sectors is viewed as
different from, and less dangerous than, work in industry, or

because vested interests have successfuly fought off attempts at a broader extension of social protection.

Other problems arise from an inadequate inspectorate allied to the complexity of existing rules and regulations, or the lack of a clear delineation of responsibility for their enforcement. In some countries, for example, responsibility for the enforcement of child labour laws is divided between the Health and Safety Inspectorate, the Public Health Inspection Services, Education and the Police. It would thus appear that the most important areas for action in industrialized countries are the wider application of national legislation, the rationalization of existing regulations, a clear delineation of the powers and duties of inspectorates, and the enhancement of the regulatory and enforcement machinery of the state.

While a strengthening of the inspectorate is clearly vital, prominence should also be given to public information campaigns to promote awareness, firstly that the problem exists, and secondly of the laws and regulations themselves. As we have seen, it is not only those in developing countries who are loath to acknowledge the existence, or at least the extent, of the child labour problem. Public education campaigns against child labour originated in industrialized countries in the last century and they still have not outlived their usefulness. However, when we turn to the developing world the picture is both complex and sobering. Here we encounter a heterogeneous group of countries (from China and India to Sierra Leone and Haiti) at different levels of development and with varying resource endowments and capabilities. Over the last 20 years there have been pertinent and remarkable achievements in education. For example, according to UNESCO, the school enrolment ratio for children between 6 and 11 years of age in Africa doubled between 1960 and 1985 – from 32.7 per cent in 1960 to 65.9 per cent in 1985; in Asia the ratio rose from 57.7 per cent to 83.5 per cent (Bequele, 1986, pp. 35–6). Countries such as Sri Lanka, Kenya and Tanzania have already achieved, or are fast approaching, universal primary education.

When we look at the participation of girls in the school system, seen by the World Bank as one of the best investments for development, the picture is even more remarkable. In 1960, the average rate of female enrolment in primary schools in the developing world was 30 per cent. Today, it is more than 80 per cent. And apart from the achievement of China, where almost 100 per cent of girls now attend primary schools, the rate of female enrolment has also doubled, or almost doubled, in Bangladesh, Ethiopia, Nepal, Somalia, Zaire, Mozambique, Tanzania, Sudan, Ghana, Kenya, Zambia, Papua New Guinea, Morocco, Tunisia, Syria, Algeria, Iran, Iraq and Libya. According to Peter Adamson: '. . . this has a fair claim to being regarded as one of the great achievements of the last quarter of a century.' (*New Internationalist*, October 1986, p. 19). However, the picture in many other countries is less inspiring with declining education and health expenditures compared with rising defence spending (see figure 7.1).

Such trends should also be seen in relation to the sheer size of the child population in many developing countries. Table 7.1 shows that between 40 per cent and 50 per cent of the population may be under 15 years of age. Such child population growth in recent years has meant that the absolute number of children outside of the school system has actually increased. Between 1960 and 1975 the total number of children in the developing world aged between 6 and 11 not attending school rose from 110 million to 121 million (UN

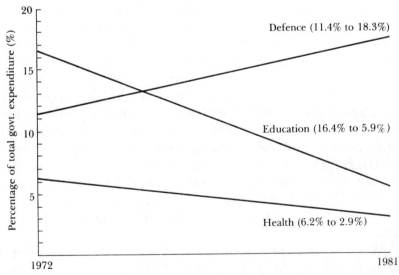

Figure 7.1   Investment in human resources in the developing world, 1972–81

Source: UNICEF State of the World's Children 1985, The World Bank, 1984

Department of International Economic and Social Affairs, 1979, p. 15). This increase is even more for Africa and Asia, for rural areas, and for girls. Even using UNESCO ratios for school enrolments in 1985 this still leaves 28 per cent of children aged between 6 and 11 years, and about 54 per cent of those between 12 and 17 years, not in school and who may well be in the labour force and working (Bequele, 1986, p. 36). Such discussion of ratios and absolute enrolment tells one nothing of the quality of the education service, which itself has contributed, according to the World Bank, significantly to the failure of coverage and retention of poor children.

This uneven progress must be taken into account in formulating realistic policies on child labour. Those countries which have achieved significant socio-economic progress and virtually achieved universal primary education could attain the objective of abolishing child labour without too much difficulty. With the acceleration of secondary education, the effective minimum age of entry to employment could be raised from around 12 years – which it is at present – to about 15 years. Additionally, these countries should aim at extending the sectoral coverage of their national legislation and at

Table 7.1 Children as a proportion of population

Country	Population 1982 (millions)	GNP per capita ($ US) 1982	Average annual rate of growth 1970–82	% population below age 15	Population below age 15 (millions)
Brazil	127	2,240	2.4	45	57.15
China	1,196	310	1.4	38	454.5
Ethiopia	33	140	2.0	48	15.84
India	717	260	2.3	43	308.81
Kenya	18	390	4.0	51	9.18
Nigeria	91	860	2.6	50	45.5
Sri Lanka	15	320	1.7	40	6.0
UK	56	9,660	0.1	23	12.88
USA	232	13,160	1.0	23	56.36

Source: The World Bank, World Development Report 1984, Oxford University Press

strengthening their enforcement machinery. By contrast, the situation in most developing countries, especially those termed 'least developed', is different both in terms of the scale of the problem and in the scope for action. In these countries, the size of the task, and the need for greater effort, have to be balanced against the real constraints facing them. There are, however, measures which even countries at low levels of development can take, particularly in the provision of services and the extension of basic production.

Though almost all countries have adopted national minimum age laws for admission to employment and conditions to regulate the nature of child work, these laws are seldom adequately implemented. There are several reasons for this. National laws may be unrealistic, with their sectoral coverage way beyond a country's institutional and enforcement capacity. But, then, enforcement becomes meaningless in the absence of opportunities for schooling. Where the education system is not adequately developed, it is neither possible nor sensible to consider total coverage or enforcement. As we have seen, in many if not most countries world-wide, the labour inspectorate is inadequately staffed and ill-equipped to carry out its legal responsibilities. The inspectorate is besides often hampered by problems of verification. Small enterprises employing children are generally unlicensed and unregistered and do not usually keep a record of their employees. Even if they did, it may still be difficult to verify the ages of children since in many developing countries birth certificates are a relatively recent innovation. For these reasons, countries should initially adopt a pragmatic approach, which sets realistic and attainable goals. A low-income country should focus on selected areas and sectors which exhibit the most abuses of child labour. In effect, public policy should in the beginning take urban areas as its focus, with an emphasis on industry and mining, gradually extending its coverage to other sectors. This mirrors the ILO stance on priorities, as put to me in their Lima Regional Office in 1985. UNICEF, too, with its emphasis on street children, reinforces this general view that it is sensible to concentrate on the urban areas first. It also accords with government perceptions. But, whatever their level of advancement, developing countries should articulate certain imperatives in their national laws and should ensure they are observed.

First and foremost should be the identification and prohibition of child work in dangerous activities. Large numbers of children are still found working with toxic substances in agriculture, or are working in dangerous industries such as mining, metal work, glass manufacturing, matches and fireworks. There is little doubt that employment in the armed forces can be dangerous to one's health too! Work which so endangers the health and safety of children is clearly totally unacceptable and must be strictly prohibited in all countries whatever their level of development. Allied to these public policy goals should be an emphasis upon the protection of the youngest and most vulnerable children. A country should aim, as a short-term objective, at ensuring that children under, say, 12 years of age do not work. Many countries have the capacity to ban child employment before the completion of compulsory primary education, or 12 years of age. Such a measure would at least meet the lower age limit set by Convention 138 and would almost immediately significantly reduce the incidence of child labour and provide protection to the youngest and most vulnerable groups.

Education laws are the best child labour laws; and the single most important instrument for ensuring that children under 12 years of age do not work, is the expansion of primary education. Here much needs to be done to reduce class, gender, ethnic and regional disparities in access to education. The real economic cost of schooling to the poor must also be reduced. Education is a social right and the poor should not be disadvantaged by the direct and indirect costs of schooling. These costs include direct costs such as school fees, but also the additional costs of uniforms, materials and meals; though the most important cost for poor parents is the opportunity cost of sending to school children who could be contributing to the family budget. As child workers can contribute as much as 30 per cent to household incomes this illustrates how unrealistic and harmful attempts to abolish child work at a stroke would be in the absence of compensating income and employment adjustments and, of course, schools. In the short term, school feeding programmes and other measures could reduce the burden on poor families and make it more attractive to send their children to school rather than to work.

Without sufficient political will, issues to do with labour and human rights and the promotion of equal opportunities will easily be set aside. Enlightened public policy in this area will need careful nurturing from both inside and outside government. It is well known that the social ministries, such as education, labour, health and welfare, often become marginalized in policy and budgetary allocation debates. The reasons for this are obvious: social objectives are elusive and their economic returns are difficult to demonstrate; they are considered to be a heavy burden on the exchequer; and when they do not exist, they are not missed because the negative impact of inaction is often not felt immediately and dramatically, as for say a balance-of-payments problem. If social ministries are to exert greater influence on resource allocation their programmes must be designed to be cost-effective and to be seen to contribute to the attainment of multiple social goals. For example, the expansion of education and welfare programmes could be carried out in areas exhibiting a high level and incidence of child labour. Educational reforms could be linked to labour utilization patterns. For example, in many countries school calendars are still tied to colonial models but they could be adapted to suit household labour requirements during the planting and harvesting seasons. In this way, children could both attend school during slack periods and assist their families during peak labour periods. The same point has been made in connection with urban schools and the needs of street children.

Clearly, child labour touches on a number of ministries. In addition to labour, education, health and welfare ministries, it involves those concerned with the implementation of income and employment generating programmes and community development programmes. Therefore, in so far as local conditions require it, an inter-agency co-ordinating body on child labour may be usefully established, with a view to exerting pressure within government and ensuring the effective delivery of services for the reduction of child labour and the protection of working children.

The public agenda is a reflection of the balance of social forces obtaining in a society. And workers, employees and non-governmental organizations can, through pressure, influence the shape and thrust of society goals. Workers organizations have a special role and a largely untapped potential in this area. Firstly, they can initiate and facilitate the organization of especially vulnerable groups of workers. Secondly, they can carry out extensive educational and information campaigns on the evils and consequences of child labour, and can encourage positive action locally, nationally and internationally. Thirdly, they can serve as a watchdog for the observance of international and national labour standards. Fourthly, they can identify work situations in which child abuse occurs. Finally, they can extend the scope of their social and welfare services so that child workers are included among the target groups which receive direct support from them. And yet, trade union interest and action in this area has in the past been generally limited; there is much ground to be made up. Trade unions have a key role to play in any integrated child labour campaigns which take the raising of public awareness as the central objective. International organizations, such as ILO, UNICEF and WHO, have a role and a duty to assist such actions, notwithstanding government sensitivities; they must be mindful of Burke's admonition too. They have a responsibility to raise the profile of child labour within their own organizations and to educate member states to place the issue higher on their agenda.

For many child labour is not simply a neglected public policy issue, it is a human rights concern. As Patrick Montgomery comments: 'Few human rights abuses are as widely and unanimously condemned, while at the same time being as universally practised, as the exploitation of child labour' (Montgomery, 1985, p. 3). And as the MRG report reminds us: 'There is still no effective guarantee of children's rights in the international arena' (Boyden, 1985, p. 9). In this final section the more contentious ethical issues raised by child labour need to be explored. The notion of children's rights only emerged in the West in the early nineteenth century, when childhood came to be widely recognized as a separate status requiring special measures of protection. Earlier laws such as the Roman *patria potestas* doctrine treated children as parental, and usually paternal, property. The gradual abandonment of such notions was a necessary prerequisite for the recognition of the child as an individual possessing both rights and duties. Such a shift was manifest through efforts to proide for child welfare and to bolster the responsibility of the family for the well-being of the child. The nineteenth century saw the advent of measures to curtail the exploitation of child labour, to provide basic education, to ensure some form of financial support for dependent children and for parents in extreme cases of neglect and abuse.

However, these measures were not designed to promote the notion that children are the autonomous holders of rights in the same way as adults, but rather to define more clearly the rights and duties of parents (Alston, 1986, p. 2). As John Stuart Mill made quite clear, his philosophy of rights was: '. . . meant to apply to human beings in the maturity of their faculties. We are not speaking of children, or young persons below the age which the law may fix as that of manhood or womanhood. Those who are still in a state to require being taken care of by others, must be protected against their own actions as well as against external injury' (Alston, 1986, p. 2).

The first comprehensive international instrument in the field – the Geneva Declaration of the Rights of the Child, was adopted in 1924 by the Assembly of the League of Nations. The Declaration, inspired by the Englishwoman Eglantyne Jebb, was cast in terms of duties declared and accepted by men and women of all nations, and according to which the child must be given the means requisite for its normal development, both materially and spiritually. The League's Declaration was the first official recognition of a common human concern which had previously been relegated to parents and philanthropists. But it only lasted as long as the League and was not resurrected until 1959, in the form of the Declaration of the Rights of the Child, adopted by the United Nations on 20 November 1959. It remains the most important statement on children's rights:

1 The right to equality, regardless of race, colour, sex, religion, national or social origin.
2 The right to develop physically and mentally in a healthy manner.
3 The right to a name and nationality.
4 The right to adequate nutrition, housing and medical services.
5 The right to special care, if handicapped.
6 The right to love, understanding and protection.
7 The right to free education, to play and recreation.
8 The right to be among the first to receive relief in times of disaster.
9 The right to protection against all forms of neglect, cruelty and exploitation.
10 The right to be brought up in a spirit of tolerance, peace and universal brotherhood.

However, the Declaration is concerned with generalized principles or moral entitlenments and does not extend to children's enabling rights. It is not a legally binding instrument and there exists no enforcement mechanism. In fact, the rights set out in the Declaration are by no means the only ones recognized for children by the international community. Over 80 conventions, declarations and other binding and non-binding international instruments contain provisions that explicitly or implicitly apply to children. As a body of international law defining the rights of children, this heterogeneous collection is totally unsatisfactory, both in terms of its in-built incoherence and because of the vast areas not covered (Cantwell, 1986, p. 9).

The initiative of the government of Poland (they had also proposed the 1924 Declaration and the founding of UNICEF) on the eve of IYC (1979) to formulate a Convention on the Rights of the Child – a potentially binding instrument – seemed welcomed. The open-ended Working Group, set up by the UN Commission on Human Rights to produce a draft text of the Convention, has met for a week each year since 1979 and has a maximum membership of 43. Cantwell has drawn attention to some of the 'wobbly standards' so far built into the text that lower, or ignore, standards contained in other international instruments (as, for example, children in armed conflict) (Cantwell, 1986, p. 10). But the major problem has been the poor input into the drafting by developing countries. Just 15 countries represented the developing world in 1986 and less than half of these attended regularly, and even fewer participated in any significant way. This began to change in 1987 and 1988 with a significant input by India. Interestingly, UNICEF has taken a lower public profile throughout, preferring to exercise influence through support of the NGOs. Following completion of the first draft and second reading in 1988, the target date for adoption of 1989 seems attainable.

Article 38 covers child labour and it was following the 1985 meeting of the UN Working Group that Poland revised its original proposal for this article, deleting reference to protection from all forms of discrimination, social exploitation or degradation of dignity and also dropping any specific mention of trafficking in children. The NGOs were concerned that Article 18 failed to deal with sexual exploitation and trafficking. These points were taken up at the 1986 Working Group and provisionally adopted as below:

Article 18

1   The States Parties to the present Convention recognize the right of the child to be protected from economic exploitation and from performing any work that is likely to be hazardous

or to interfere with the child's education, or to be harmful to the child's health or physical, mental, spiritual, moral or social development.

2   The States Parties to the present Convention shall take legislative and administrative measures to ensure the implementation of this article. To this end, and having regard to the relevant provisions of other international instruments, the States Parties shall in particular:

(a)   provide for a minimum age or minimum ages for admission to employment;

(b)   provide for appropriate regulation of the hours and conditions of employment; and

(c)   provide for appropriate penalties or other sanctions to ensure the effective enforcement of this article.

The text as adopted seems acceptable to the ILO who have been perhaps the most effective UN participant throughout. A very positive inclusion is the reference in paragraph 1 to 'any work', which is of course much wider than 'employment' or 'occupation', covering as it does any activity, in whatever context, in which the child engages or is engaged whether for remuneration or other reward. The reference in paragraph 2 to other international instruments makes it clear that the provisions of this article are not exclusive. There is no doubt that certain other standards could, none the less, be mentioned, especially using the formulation of ideas expressed in the conclusions and recommendations of the UN Seminar. The Seminar had defined 'employment in armed conflict' as hazardous work. NGOs pointed out that the ILO Convention 138 stipulated that children under 18 should in no circumstances be permitted to undertake hazardous work. The point failed to be appreciated by states who are not particularly sympathetic to the Geneva Protocols because of the rights it accords to terrorists. As it stands, Article 20 downgrades the provisions set out in the Geneva Conventions, whereby for those in the 15 to 18 age group, states are urged to give priority to recruiting the older members of that group into their armed forces. Full discussion regarding implementation lies ahead. The USA has already said that only those states that ratify the Convention should contribute to the cost. Since the USA is unlikely to ratify the Convention, this condition would undoubtedly reduce its effectiveness.

We have proceeded so far without questioning the whole notion of children's rights, as if this was unproblematic. Nothing could be farther from the truth as the concept is often viewed as lacking precision. In relation to human rights provisions in general, rights accorded to children may:

Reaffirm or reflect rights granted to human beings of whatever age, for example, protection from torture, the right to a name and nationality, the right to social security.

Improve, with regard to children, the standards applicable to human beings in general, for example, special conditions of employment, administration of juvenile justice, conditions of deprivation of liberty.

Address issues that are solely or more especially relevant to children, for example, adoption, primary education, contact with parents.

Most of the human rights of children fall into the second and third of the above categories: they raise the standard of, or add to, rights afforded to human beings in general. They do so in order to take account of the particular needs of children as especially vulnerable, essentially dependent and developing human beings.

Human rights are traditionally classified under five headings: civil, political, economic, social and cultural. Although special, children's rights are an integral part of human rights, and they can also be classified in this way, except that the very status of a child means in principle that he or she has no political rights. Thus:

The civil rights of chidren include the right to a name and national-ity, protection from torture and maltreatment, special rules governing the circumstances and conditions under which children may be deprived of their liberty or separated from their parents, etc.

The economic rights of children include the right to benefit from social security, the right to a standard of living adequate to ensure proper development, and protection from exploitation at work.

The social rights of children include the right to the highest attainable standard of health and access to medical services, the right to special care for handicapped children, protection from sexual exploitation and abduction and the regulation of adoption.

The cultural rights of children include the right to education, access
to appropriate information, recreation and leisure, and participation in artistic and cultural activities.

Another way of grouping rights is to talk about the three 'Ps':
provision, *protection* and *participation*. In other words, the right to
possess, receive or have access to certain things or services, the right
to be shielded from certain acts and practices, and the right to do
things, express oneself and have an effective voice in matters affecting
one's life. There are usually elements of the three 'Ps' in each of the
traditional categories. Thus, for examples, social rights include the
right to receive medical care, the right to be protected from exploitation, and the right to have one's opinions taken into account.

Both methods of classification are useful in analysing and
understanding children's rights. One classification shows us, for
example, that children have no political rights. The other highlights
the fact that they have very few rights with regard to participation.
We can also see that the criticism sometimes levelled against the
concept and content of children's rights – that they are essentially
paternalistic and over-protective – has no real grounds. Protection is
only one element among others as a basis for children's rights.
Indeed, it is a feature that is no less important in overall human
rights provisions, and in those concerning special groups such as
ethnic, linguistic or religious minorities, than it is with regard to
children.

The question is often posed as to the extent to which human rights
can be truly universal, given the wide range of socio-economic,
religious and cultural realities throughout the world. Is it possible
and useful, then, to set out standards that are applicable and applied
world-wide? The problem is apparently compounded when it comes
to the human rights of children. First of all, it is said, there are
significantly divergent perceptions from one country to another
regarding both the age at which childhood ends, and the child's role
in the family and society. The fact that methods of upbringing and
socialization vary greatly is also seen as a major obstacle to drawing
up global rules governing the treatment of children. Is the
formulation of an international set of children's rights a feasible and
worthwhile proposition?

The issues raised here have to be taken into account, but should
not detract from the clear evidence that, notwithstanding differences

in culture, ideology and level of economic wealth, a whole range of children's rights are fundamentally shared by all peoples. Ways of achieving them may differ, and they may individually require or be given different priority according to time and place, but they remain indivisible pre-conditions for the child's harmonious and full development.

Nevertheless, since the 1970s there has been a continuing debate between 'liberationists' and 'protectionists', with these two broad schools of thought being defined as 'those interested in protecting children and those interested in protecting children's rights ...' (Franklin, 1986, p. 17 after Farson, 1973). One school has stressed that children require protection by special rights tailored to their needs as children. But as Freeman states, 'How can you talk about rights inherent in people who are unable to exercise them? Instead, we should be concerned with requiring adults to meet their obligations or duties' (Freeman 1983, p. 38). In opposition is the view that children should have the same rights as adults '. . . of whatever age, who wants to make use of them' (Holt, 1975, p 15).

Like many polar opposites there is considerable overlap between the two, and they can be viewed as complementary. If children are given the right to work, as Holt, Farson and others support, they, like adults, will require protection from poor and dangerous working conditions, but this should not erode their autonomy and choice in other matters (Franklin, 1986, pp. 17–18). In advocating the right to work, Holt is seeking to offer a choice and not impose an obligation for there is a vast difference (as Victorian Britain shows) between being obliged to work and having the right to work.

For the liberationists, protectionism can easily translate itself into paternalism, thus:

> Despite the evidence of a high capacity of children in the Third World for social and economic independence, few reformers are sufficiently free from their paternalism to press for a genuinely greater autonomy and self-organization of working children. (Goddard and White, 1982, p. 472)

These philosophical distinctions abound in the child labour field as few can bring themselves to take an absolutist stance and say all child work is bad. For Karl Marx: '. . . every child whatever, from the age of 9 years, ought to become a productive labourer . . ., in conformity to the general law of nature, viz: to work in order to be able to eat, and work not only with the brain but with the hands too' (quoted in Padover, (ed.), 1975, p. 91). According to Marx, children of working people could be divided into three classes: 9 to 12, 13 to 15 and 16 to 17 years who ought to work in any workshop or household for two, four and six hours respectively. Marx reflected the protectionist ethos of his age in believing that, 'the rights of children and juvenile persons must be vindicated. They are unable to act for themselves. It is, therefore, the duty of society to act on their behalf' (Padover (ed.), 1975, p. 92). It was through the creative combination of education and work, in ways pioneered by Robert Owen, that the working class would, according to Marx, be raised above the level of the higher and middle classes. This Marx most clearly states in his *Critique of the Gotha Programme*:

A general prohibition of child labour is incompatible with the existence of large-scale industry and hence an empty, pious wish. Its realization – if it were possible – would be reactionary, since with a strict regulation of the working time according to the different age groups and other safety measures for the protection of children, an early combination of productive labour with education is one of the most potent means for the transformation of present-day society. (Marx and Engels, 1968, p. 334)

If paternalism is a trap to be avoided, some, like Boyden and Hudson, stress the advancement of children's interests through the mechanism of self-advocacy, in which children with common problems unite to promote their cause (Boyden and Hudson, 1985, p. 10). We have already mentioned examples of self-advocacy in relation to street children in Latin America and child workers in India. Additionally, we could point to the protest of Filipino school children against child prostitution (Boyden and Hudson, 1985, p. 11). Nick Van Hear has graphically shown in Ghana the potential children have in resisting exploitation (1982, p. 449–514). Despite the rapid expansion of schooling in Ghana since the 1950s, children are still widely employed in agriculture, particularly in the North. The development of commercial agriculture has increased the use of hired labour, especially that of children. Van Hear's study of the rice industry in North Ghana explored the extent to which children were increasingly drawn into industry as village men became conscious of their exploitation and withdrew to expand their own farms. But, with a growing labour shortage from the mid-1970s, these casual child workers had their bargaining position strengthened. This resulted in children taking collective action against farmers who tried to cheat workers and to extract more work for less pay. Such action included sit-down strikes, go-slows, and even threats of violence. The worst farmers were boycotted. Children in this case were able to act collectively to restrict their utilization and exploitation. In contrast to the partial success of such resistance, legislation in Ghana has signally failed to improve the welfare of child workers, in part because of the involvement of civil servants and members of the government in capitalist farming. Such examples only touch the surface in terms of what children may be capable of in the sphere of self-advocacy and collective action, and this has led Boyden and Hudson to demand that: 'strenuous efforts should be made at national and international level to support self-advocacy, self-representation and autonomous organizations for children' (p. 13). But this inevitably entails some orchestration by adults.

Much of the libertarian approach to children's rights turns on the notion that children should not be treated as a special category, but should share the rights adults enjoy. If children work, they should have the right to join trade unions. This approach finds expression in Morice:

> ... on the one hand it is desirable that children, in common with all human beings, but especially in view of their physical limitations, should benefit from laws forbidding their exploitation; however, to reduce the problem of child work to one of 'protection' is to exclude children from any decisions about themselves and to create inferior beings. In our view, the only acceptable 'protection' ... lies in giving children the right to be heard and to organize; up to now, this right has been immediately and violently repressed when children have claimed it. (Morice, 1981, p. 157)

White suggests that if one goes beyond crude abolitionist views to positions which accept the notion that work of all kinds is not necessarily harmful to children, and instead focus on the labour element of exploitation due to their status as minors in society, we

reach a paradoxical and ambiguous position (White, 1985, p. 9). We believe that children are more exploited because of their status; on the other hand, most of the interventions adults construct to protect working children perpetuate their special, separate status. White goes on to suggest that, though there may be reasons why some aspects of the struggle for better working conditions for children should be separated from general labour struggles, much more might be achieved if working children could be assisted in securing basic workers' rights as Morice argues.

The earlier discussion of the nature of children's rights provides a useful framework and enables one to steer between the supposed alternatives of protection and self-advocacy. The three elements of provision, protection and participation suggest certain basic principles to guide the construction of programmes for working children.

In the provision of services to working children the objective should be to promote their integrated physical, mental and social development. Such an approach moves from the simple reaction to emergency needs towards a more creative provision of assistance. Ways of combining work and education with flexible schooling and relevant curricula, clearly offer considerable potential, as can be seen in pilot programmes in Latin America.

Protection will still be needed in those areas of priority concern, namely the super-exploitation found in the sex and drugs industry; in hazardous industries, within military service, etc. But finally we must recognize that children can be the agents of change and not simply its object. Children have the right to self-expression and action and have a potential role in the planning and execution of programmes. The vast and complex nature of child labour implies a multi-faceted approach, for there is clearly no one set of interventions which deal effectively with the problem (Bequele and Boyden, 1988, p. 22). Clearly the balance and emphasis between these three elements will be determined by the nature of the social context and the stage of development of the children concerned. That said, more attention needs to be given to the under-utilized potential for self-advocacy

A children's demonstration on the issue of children's rights, Lima, Peru
(*Source*: Mauricio Audibert)

'Do we know what we want?' Part of a public awareness campaign
on children's rights, Lima, Peru
Source: TIPACOM (Talleres Infantiles Proyectados a la Comunidad)

that certainly appears manifest among older children in urban areas.

What is not in doubt is that the persistence of child labour is an affront to our conscience, and that the effective abolition of child labour is a challenge to the international community. A global partnership to take up this challenge still appears remote given the pervasive perception of the issue as a low priority concern. Thirty years after the 1959 Declaration and ten years after the IYC would seem an appropriate juncture to re-focus world attention on this neglected issue. But such an interest in anniversaries is likely to be lost on those millions of children who are still constrained to work at the cost of their health and development. We must therefore never forget that though many things can wait, children cannot. For this and many other reasons, it is time that children had priority in the development process.

Bibliography

Allen, E. E. 1981: Testimony before the Committee on the Judiciary United States Senate 1981, by Ernest E. Allen, Chairman of Jefferson County Task Force on Child Prostitution and Pornography.

Alston, P. 1986: 'Children's rights: a role for UNICEF'. Unpublished paper.

Agnelli, S. 1986: *Street Children: A Growing Urban Tragedy*. London: Weidenfeld and Nicolson.

Ariès, P. 1962: *Centuries of Childhood: A Social History of Family Life*. New York: Random House.

Anti-Slavery Society 1978: Child labour in Morocco's carpet industry.

Anti-Slavery Society 1983: Child lahour in South Africa.

Anti-Slavery Society 1984a: Child domestic workers in Latin America. Report to the United Nations Working Group on Slavery, unpublished manuscript.

Anti-Slavery Society 1984b: Children in especially difficult circumstances: child labour. Report for UNICEF, unpublished manuscript.

Anti-Slavery Society 1984c: Child labour on plantations. Unpublished paper for Commission on Human Rights, tenth session.

Anti-Slavery Society 1985: Children in especially difficult circumstances: street children. Report for UNICEF, unpublished manuscript.

Banerjee, S. 1979: *Child Labour in India*. London: The Anti-Slavery Society.

Banerjee, S. 1980: *Child Labour in Thailand*. London: The Anti-Slavery Society.

Bequele, A. 1984: *Towards an Action Programme on Child Labour*. Geneva, ILO.

Bequele, A. 1985: Child labour: trends, problems and policies. In Shah (ed.), *Child Labour: A Threat to Health and Development*. Geneva: Defence for Children International.

Bequele, A. 1986: Child Labour: A framework for policies and programmes. In *Child Labour: A Briefing Manual*, Geneva: ILO.

Bequele, A. and Boyden, J. 1988: *Combating Child Labour*, Geneva: ILO.

Berrington, G. 1985: Working Paper produced for the International Seminar on Child Labour.

Blanchard, F. 1979: *Declaration by the Director-General of the ILO concerning the International Year of the Child*. Geneva: ILO.

Blanchard, F. 1983: *Report of the Director-General*. Geneva: ILO.

Boudhiba, A. 1982: Exploitation of child labour. Final Report of the Special Rapporteur of the UN Sub-Commission on Prevention of Discrimination and Protection of Minorities. Geneva: UN.

Boyden, J. and Hudson, A. 1985: *Children's Rights and Responsibilities*. London: The Minority Rights Group.

Bygrave, M. 1986: On the streets where they live, in *The Sunday Times Magazine*. 2 February.

Campagna, D. 1985: The economics of juvenile prostitution in the USA. In *International Children's Rights Monitor*, vol. 2, no. 1.

Cantwell, N. 1986: Children's rights in an adult society. In *Future*, 18–19, UNICEF Regional Office for South Central Asia.

Challis, J. and Elliman, D. 1979: *Child Workers Today*. London: Quartermaine House.

Child Workers in Asia Support Group 1985: *Child Workers in Asia*, vol. 1, no. 1.

Child Workers in Asia Support Group 1986a: *Child Workers in Asia*, vol. 2, no. 1.

Child Workers in Asia Support Group 1986b: *Child Workers in Asia*, vol. 2, no. 2.

Child Workers in Asia Support Group 1986c: *Child Workers in Asia*, vol. 2, no. 3.

Child Workers in Asia Support Group 1987: *Child Workers in Asia*, vol. 3, no. 1.

Cole, S. 1980: *Working Kids on Working*. New York: Lothrop, Lee and Shepard.

Collins, P. 1965: *Dickens & Education*. London: Macmillan.

Croll, E. 1984: 'The New Peasant Household Economy in China'. The Hague: Institute of Social Studies.

Cunningham, H. 1985: Slaves or savages: some attitudes to labouring children *c*.1780–1870. Unpublished paper, University of Kent.

Cunningham, H. 1987: Child labour in the industrial revolution. In *The Historian*, no. 14.

Davin, A. 1982: Child labour, the working class family and domestic ideology in 19th-century Britain. In *Development and Change*, vol. 13, no. 4. London: Sage Publications.

Dodge, C. 1987: *War, Violence and Children in Uganda*. Oxford University Press.

Elson, D. 1982: The differentiation of children's labour in the capitalist labour market. In *Development and Change*, vol. 13, no. 4. London: Sage Publications.

Engels, F. 1926. *Condition of the Working Class in England in 1844*. London: George Allen and Unwin.

Ennew, J. 1985a: Juvenile street workers in Lima, Peru. Unpublished report for the Overseas Development Administration and the Anti-Slavery Society.

Ennew, J. 1985b: Child soldiers: serving or working? *International Children's Rights Monitor*, vol. 2, no. 2.

Ennew, J. 1986a: *The Sexual Exploitation of Children*. Cambridge: Polity Press.

Ennew, J. 1986b: Children of the street. In *The New Internationalist*, no. 164.

Franklin, B. (ed.) 1986: *The Rights of Children*. Oxford: Basil Blackwell.

Freire, P. 1985: *Pedagogy of the Oppressed*. London: Pelican.

Fyfe, A. 1985: *All Work And No Play: Child Labour Today*. London: Trades Union Congress.

Goddard, V. and White, B. 1982: Child workers and capitalist development: an introductory note and bibliography. In *Development and Change*, vol. 13, no. 4, London: Sage Publications.

Harriman, E. 1984: Modern slavery, *New Statesman*, 10 February.

Hayes, D. 1985: Conscription Conflict. Helsinki: International Peace Bureau/War Resisters International.

Holt, J. 1975: *Escape from Childhood*. London: Pelican.

Ideas Forum, 1983: The exploitation of children. *UNICEF Supplement*, no. 16.

Ideas Forum, 1984. Abandoned and street children. *UNICEF Supplement*, no. 18.

International Confederation of Free Trade Unions, 1986: *Breaking Down the Wall of Silence: How to Combat Child Labour*. Brussels.

International Labour Office, 1986: *Child Labour: A Briefing Manual*. Geneva.

International Labour Office, 1988: Conditions of work digest: the emerging response to child labour, vol. 7:1. Geneva.

Jenks, C. 1982: *The Sociology of Childhood*. London: Batsford.

Jomo, K. S., Zainie, J., Ramasamy, P. and Suppiah, S. 1984: Early labour: children at work on Malaysian plantations, Kuala Lumpur. London: INSAN and ASS.

Liégeois, J. 1987: *Gypsies and Travellers*. Strasbourg: Council of Europe.

Lloyd, R. 1985: Working Paper produced for 1985 International Seminar.

Longford, M. 1985: Working Paper for 1985 International Seminar.

Kayongo-Male, D. and Walji, P. 1984: *Children at Work in Kenya*. Nairobi: Oxford University Press.

MacLennan, E. 1982: Child Labour in London. London: Low Pay Unit.

MacLennan, E. et al. 1985: *Working Children*. London: Low Pay Unit.

MacLennan, E. 1986: Children's rights at work. In Franklin (ed.) *The Rights of Children*. Oxford: Basil Blackwell.

Marx, K. 1968. Critique of Gotha Programme. In Karl Marx and Frederich Engels, *Selected Works*. London: Lawrence and Wishart.

Mayhew, H. 1985: London Labour and the London Poor. London: Penguin.

Mendelievich, E. (ed.), 1979: *Children at Work*. Geneva: ILO.

Mitra, A. 1984: The firework kids. *New Internationalist*, no. 138, p. 4.

Montgomery, P. 1985: Working Paper for International Seminar.

Moorehead, C. 1987: *School Age Workers in Britain Today*. London: Anti-Slavery Society.

Morice, A. 1981: The exploitation of children in the informal sector: proposals for research. In Rodgers, G. and Standing, G.; *Child Work, Poverty and Underdevelopment*. Geneva: ILO.

Newsweek, 1983: All work and no play. 24 January.

Onyango, P. 1985a, 1984–5: *Progress Report on Child Labour and Health Project in Kenya*. University of Nairobi.

Onyango, P. 1985b: Africa: The child labour situation. In *Child Labour: A Threat to Health and Development*. Geneva: DCI.

Onyango, P. 1988: Child labour policies and programmes in Kenya. In Bequele and Boyden 1988.

Padover, S. (ed.) 1985: *Karl Marx on Education, Women and Children*. New York: McGraw Hill.

Platt, A. 1969: The child savers: the invention of delinquency. Chicago: University of Chicago Press.

Puxon, G. 1987: *Roma: Europe's Gypsies*. London: Minority Rights Group.

Rodgers, G. and Standing, G. (eds) 1981: *Child Work, Poverty and Under-development*, Geneva: ILO.

Rosen, R. 1982: *The Lost Sisterhood: Prostitution in America 1900–1918*. Baltimore and London: The Johns Hopkins Press.

Rosenblatt, R. 1984: *Children of War*. New York: Anchor Press.

Schorsch, A. 1979: *Images of Childhood: An Illustrated Social History*. New York: Main Street Press.

Searight, S. 1980: *Child Labour in Spain*. London: Anti-Slavery Society.

Sereny, G. 1984: *The Invisible Children: A Study of Child Prostitution*. London: André Deutsch.

Shah, P. and Cantwell, N. (eds) 1985: *Child Labour: A Threat to Health and Development*. Geneva: DCI.

Standing, G. 1982: State policy and child labour: accommodation versus legitimation. In *Development and Change*, vol. 13, no. 4. London: Sage Publications.

Thompson, E. 1984: *The Making of the English Working Class*. London: Pelican.

Tyler, A. 1988: Little beggars. In *The Independent Magazine*, 3 December.

UNICEF, 1984: *The State of the World's Children Report 1985*. Oxford University Press.

UNICEF, 1985: The Exploitation of Working and Street Children. Unpublished draft paper for the Executive Board 1986 Session. New York.

UNICEF, 1986a: Children in especially difficult circumstances. Unpublished paper for the Executive Board 1986 Session. New York.

UNICEF, 1986b: Children in situations of armed conflict. Unpublished paper for the Executive Board 1986 Session. New York.

UNICEF, 1986c: Exploitation of working and street children. Unpublished paper for the Executive Board 1986 Session. New York.

UNICEF, 1986d: Informal paper by Chairman of the Executive Board. New York.

United Farm Workers Union, 1985: Child labour and child abuse on the farm. In *Food and Justice*, vol. 2, no. 2.

United Nations, 1986: Seminar on ways and means of achieving the elimination of the exploitation of child labour in all parts of the world. Geneva.

Valcarenghi, M. 1981: *Child Labour in Italy*. London: Anti-Slavery Society.

Van Hear, N. 1982: Child labour and the development of capitalist agriculture in Ghana. *Development and Change*, vol. 13, no. 4. London: Sage Publications.

Walvin, J. 1982: *A Child's World: A Social History of English Childhood 1800–1914*. Harmondsworth: Penguin.

White, B. (ed.) 1982: Child workers. Special issue of *Development and Change*, London: Sage Publications.

White, B. 1985: The use and abuse of child and juvenile labour in developing countries: an introductory note with a focus on agriculture. Unpublished paper.

Whittaker, A. 1985: Bonded labour – India's slavery. In *The Reporter*, vol. 13, no. 2. London: Anti-Slavery Society.

Whittaker, A. 1986: Gypsy child slaves. Anti-Slavery Society. Unpublished paper.

Woods, D. 1986: Are children sold for use in war? Report from the Quaker United Nations Office, Geneva, May.

Appendix: UN Seminar 1985: Conclusions and Recommendations

Conclusions

The Seminar considers that:

(a) The exploitation of child labour is an intolerable evil which must be eliminated as a matter of the greatest urgency;

(b) The exact extent of the exploitation of child labour is not known, but it takes place in a very large number of countries throughout the world, and very many children, possibly over 100 million, are the victims of such exploitation;

(c) The exploitation of child labour takes many forms, and certain types of exploitation, for example, child prostitution and the employment of children in hazardous occupations including armed conflict, are particularly abhorrent;

(d) Certain categories of children, for example refugee or migrant children or children in countries with an *apartheid* régime, or territories under foreign occupation are particularly vulnerable to exploitation;

(e) The factors leading to the exploitation of child labour vary very widely, and include economic, social, cultural and other factors. Probably the most important causes of such exploitation are poverty and underdevelopment. For some children, work is at present an absolute necessity in order to survive;

(f) Other factors which have a bearing on the number of children at work include the general level of employment, the educational system of a country, and in particular whether, and up to what age school attendance is free and compulsory; the existence within a country of vocational training schemes, and of comprehensive legislation on the subject of child labour and the effectiveness of its enforcement; and the scope and adequacy of the needs of families of a country's social welfare and social security systems; the cultural changes that many countries are undergoing also constitute a factor influencing the number of children at work;

(g) The total elimination of all forms of exploitation of child labour throughout the world is endorsed unanimously as a long term objective. However, it will take many years to achieve. Success will depend on gradual progress in the achievement of a number of distinct short-term and medium-term programmes aimed at specific, clearly-defined, and realistic objectives;

(h) No one organization acting in isolation could hope to solve a problem of such magnitude. The elimination of the exploitation of child labour will require economic reforms aimed at a more equitable distribution of the world resources as well as the active co-operation of all those concerned with the problem, including international organizations, national Governments, local authorities, non-governmental organiza-tions at international, national and local levels, trade unions, employers, and the children themselves. Such co-operation is likely to depend on the effective mobilization of public opinion world-wide.

B   Recommendations

110. Bearing in mind the guiding principles outlined above, the Seminar makes the following recommendations:

(a) The United Nations and specialized agencies should reinforce their programmes related to the elimination of the exploitation of child labour, and in particular to the study of the economic, social, legal and cultural factors which give rise to it.

(b) States, which have not already done so, should review their legislation in the field of child labour with a view to absolute prohibition of employment of children in the following cases:

Employment before the normal age of completion of primary schooling in the country concerned;

Sexual exploitation of children for personal gratification or
   financial gain;
Night work;
Work in dangerous or unhealthy conditions;
Work concerned with trafficking in and production of illicit
   drugs;
Work involving degrading or cruel treatment.

(c) States, which have not already done so, should take the
appropriate steps to enable them to ratify ILO Convention
No. 138. In this connection, greater assistance from ILO should
be extended to the developing countries to facilitate their
increased participation in standard setting activities and in the
implementation of ratified conventions.

(d) States should, where necessary, undertake development
programmes aimed at achieving equitable distribution of
income, generating opportunities for employment, creation of
small businesses, and agrarian reforms; and:

Abolish, wherever possible, primary school fees;
Introduce flexible school time-tables to enable children who
   work to receive education;
Adapt school curricula to the preparation of a child for a
   career;
Improve the training programmes of professional workers
   dealing with child labour, in particular labour inspectors,
   social workers, and magistrates, with a view, in particular,
   to making them more sensitive to the needs of children;
Establish or improve medical services for school children and
   children at work;
Arrange for research into the effect on children of exposure to
   pesticides and other dangerous substances.

(e) States should ensure the availability of a sufficient number
of work inspectors, and train them systematically to deal with
cases of exploitation of child labour. Particular attention should
be given to national and regional plans for social and economic
development to the occupational training of young people.
National development plans should also include a section

devoted particularly to the employment of young people, and to methods of ensuring that the most deprived have sufficient resources to be able to protect themselves from conditions leading to exploitation.

(f) Special attention should be paid to the most vulnerable categories of children: children of immigrants, street children, children of minority groups including indigenous minorities, children of refugees, children in occupied territories and in countries with a régime of *apartheid*.

(g) The United Nations and specialized agencies – having regard to their special responsibilities in the field of child labour – should pay special attention to the situation which is developing dangerously for children in South Africa and in occupied Arab territories.

(h) While the question of exploitation of child labour should primarily be dealt with in the ILO, the Centre for Human Rights should continue to be concerned with this question in the framework of the rights of the child in general. The Sub-Commission should continue to have responsibility also in this field and the Working Group on Slavery should present a periodical report on progress achieved.

(i) The United Nations should give consideration to organizing a World Year (or a World Day) for the Elimination of the Exploitation of Child Labour, the essential objective of which would be to alert world public opinion.

(j) The United Nations and the specialized agencies, including the University of the United Nations, should continue to incorporate in their programmes a series of interdisciplinary and multinational projects for comparative research into the various aspects of the exploitation of child labour throughout the world and in particular in the countries of Africa, Asia and Latin America.

(k) Agencies working with community-based organizations should identify those which are concerned with child labour, and should help them in all practical ways in their task of protecting working children from exploitation.

(l) The International Labour Office should arrange for information to be provided on a regular basis by Governments and non-governmental organizations concerning the exploitation of child labour and of their experiences to eliminate or reduce it; and should submit regularly a report which should be widely circulated.

(m) UNICEF, as the designated lead agency within the United Nations for children's affairs, should be invited to examine the contribution it could make to the elimination of exploitation of child labour, particularly when reviewing its policy on "children in especially difficult circumstances" at the 1986 session of its Executive Board.

(n) All practical steps should be taken by Governments, international organizations and non-governmental organizations to increase awareness amongst children, parents, workers and employers, of the causes and the adverse effects of child labour, and measures to combat its exploitation. Such steps could include the wider dissemination of relevant international instruments translated, where appropriate into other languages in addition to the official languages of the United Nations.

(o) Support should be given to non-governmental organizations concerned with the problems of child labour, particularly at the community level, and a constructive partnership should be evolved between Governments and non-governmental organizations.

(p) Particular priority should be given to the eradication of the most abhorrent forms of child exploitation, in particular prostitution and employment in hazardous activities.

(q) The International Labour Office should take steps to encourage the effective co-operation of all agencies concerned with the elimination of exploitation of child labour, and in particular establish a framework for improved liaison between Governments, voluntary organizations, trade unions, employers and families of working children. The establishment of an international training fund could help to redress the negative effects of the outflow of skilled labour on increasing the demand for child workers.

(r) In order to reach the core of one of the prime causes of exploitation of child labour, which is poverty, increased resources should be made available through bilateral and multilateral channels for the elimination of the exploitation of child labour.

Index

Adamson, Peter, 156
adulthood, 14
Africa, 3, 11, 27, 91, 102
age hierarchy, 5, 74
Agricultural Children's Act (1867),
    33
agriculture, 26, 38–9, 73–4, 77–82,
    91, 154
  in USA, 63–7
Algeria, 71, 156
Allen, Ernest, 67
Amsterdam, 118, 154
Anti-Slavery Society, 44, 73, 76–7,
    80–2, 102–6, 114–16, 122–4,
    138, 141
apprenticeships, 17, 24, 29, 51, 73,
    96, 123, 128
Argentina, 153
Ariès, Phillipe, 12
Asia, 3, 11, 74, 102
Australia, 119

Bangladesh, 71, 74, 145, 156
Bentham, Jeremy, 150
Blanchard, Francis, 131
Bolivia, 153
bonded labour, 17, 18, 73, 75–7

Bonded Liberation Front, 76
Boswell, James, 117
Boudhiba, Abdelwahab, 2, 6, 8, 9,
    11, 14–15, 113, 133, 138
Boy Scouts, 146
Boyden, Jo, 168–9
Bracey, Heid and Janus, 70
Brazil, 9, 106–11, 149
Britain, 28–43, 128, 131, 139–44,
    150
Bulgaria, 56
Burke, Edmund, 154
Butler, Josephine, 142

California, 64–7
Campagna, Daniel, 67–9
Canada, 70
Cantwell, Nigel, 163
Centre of Concern for Child
    Labour (Bangkok), 148–9
Central America, 97
Centrepoint, 42
Chávez, César, 64–5
Chayanov, V., 74
childhood, 2, 6, 12–14, 30, 33, 58,
    141, 161, 166
ChildHope, 106